Themes On Parade

Preschool
Ages 3–5

Make every day more exciting for your little learners with great thematic ideas for

- Early Literacy
- Math
- Science
- Art
- Songs & Rhymes
- Snacktime

Plus lots more!

Written by: Jean Warren

Managing Editor: Cindy K. Daoust

Editorial Team: Becky S. Andrews, Kimberley Bruck, Gayle Bittinger, Karen P. Shelton, Diane Badden, Sharon Murphy, Kimberly Brugger-Murphy, Gerri Primak, Leanne Stratton, Allison E. Ward, Karen A. Brudnak, Sarah Hamblet, Hope Rodgers, Dorothy C. McKinney

Production Team: Lisa K. Pitts, Jennifer Tipton Cappoen (COVER ARTIST), Pam Crane, Rebecca Saunders, Chris Curry, Theresa Lewis Goode, Ivy L. Koonce, Sheila Krill, Clint Moore, Greg D. Rieves, Barry Slate, Donna K. Teal, Tazmen Carlisle, Amy Kirtley-Hill, Kristy Parton, Debbie Shoffner, Cathy Edwards Simrell, Lynette Dickerson, Mark Rainey

Table of Contents

www.themailbox.com

©2005 The Mailbox®
All rights reserved.
ISBN# 1-56234-642-3

Manufactured in the United States
10 9 8 7 6 5 4 3 2

Weather in My World

My Favorite Things

My Home

Home Decorating

Hone in on youngsters' creativity with this home-style project that is a perfect parent gift. Set out paint, crayons, and glitter glue. Give each child a tagboard copy of page 9 and have her paint or color her sign as desired. Next, encourage her to trace each letter with glitter glue. After the glue is dry, have each child name each letter and trace it with her finger. Then help her cut out the pattern and tape a length of yarn onto the back of it to make a wall hanging as shown. Have each child take her decoration home to hang in her own home, sweet home!

Build a Home

Your little builders will enjoy designing and constructing their own homes with this hands-on activity. Set out a supply of craft sticks, small twigs, pieces of straw, uncooked spaghetti, construction paper, and markers. Discuss with youngsters the different types and shapes of homes. Give each child a sheet of tagboard and ask him to choose his desired construction materials. Guide each child to construct a house shape on his tagboard and then glue it in place. Encourage him to add construction paper and marker details to complete his home. Then invite each child to share his designer home with the class.

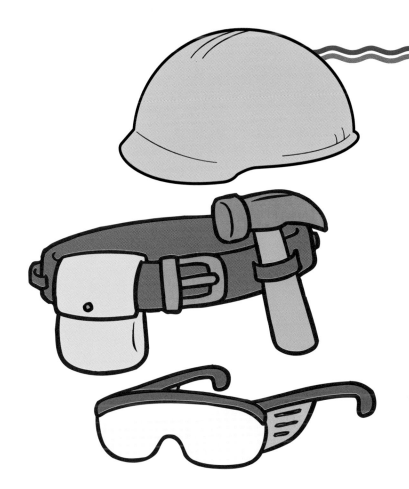

We Build a Home

Add a few construction worker props to your dramatic-play area, and you'll hear youngsters singing this catchy tune as they work. Teach students the following song and then invite several youngsters to don safety goggles, toy tool belts, and hard hats as they perform each verse. If desired, ask youngsters to help create more constructive verses for the song.

(sung to the tune "The Mulberry Bush")

This is the way we hammer the nails,
Hammer the nails, hammer the nails.
This is the way we hammer the nails
When we build our home.

This is the way we saw the wood,
Saw the wood, saw the wood.
This is the way we saw the wood
When we build our home.

Count On Your Home

Count on this center to reinforce youngsters' shape recognition and counting skills. In advance, cut different-size shapes from various colors of felt. Place the shapes and a flannelboard at a center. Invite each student in a pair to use the shapes to construct a home on the flannelboard. Have each child count the number of each different shape on his home. Next, have him count the shapes on his partner's home and compare the results. Then have the pair remove the shapes for the next home builders.

My Home

Help students understand that words make up sentences with this home-style activity. Program chart paper with the sentence starters shown. After discussing with students different types of homes, read the text aloud. Then ask a different student to complete each sentence. Record each child's word or phrase on a separate index card and add a simple drawing to illustrate each word as shown. Then attach each card to the corresponding sentence. Next, point to each word as you read each completed sentence to the class. Repeat the activity several times until each child has had a turn completing a sentence. Then place the chart and cards at a center for youngsters to experiment with words and sentences.

My Home

If I had a home,

It would have three windows

It would have one giant bed

It would have a very tiny door

It would have a green roof

And it would have a very special me

Home, Sweet Home

Youngsters will sing this catchy tune all the way home!

(sung to the tune of "Three Blind Mice")

Home, sweet home.
Home, sweet home.
No matter where you roam,
No matter where you roam.
Your home could be a hut or a tepee,
A castle, a mobile home, or a house in a tree,
But it's always a place you love to be—
Home, sweet home.

Dramatic Play

Build up youngsters' motor skills at this construction zone! Add several items—such as toy furniture, cars, dolls, and plastic animals—to your block center. Invite a few students to look at the items and then build a block home that accommodates some of the items. For example, students may build a bedroom for a doll or build a garage for a car. Then have the group explain its structure and show its special features.

Home Snack

Yum, yum! These are very tasteful homes! Give each child in a small group a plastic spoon and a graham cracker on a paper plate. Guide each youngster to break his cracker in half and place one square on his plate to be a house. Encourage him to break the other square into a shape for the roof on his house. Ask each child to scoop a spoonful of cream cheese or frosting and then spread it onto his cracker house. Provide crackers, cereal, candy, or decorating sprinkles for each youngster to use to add a door and windows to his tasty house. Then invite each child to give his house a taste test!

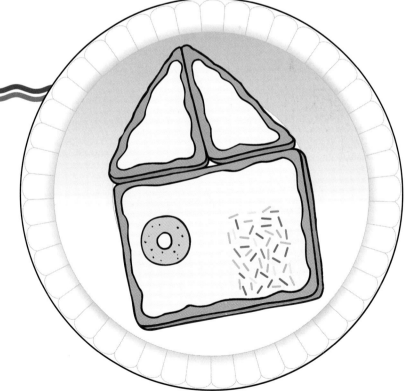

Wrapping It Up

Our Home

Build upon these constructive homemaking ideas to encourage creative and cooperative play among youngsters.

Planning the house: Locate an appliance cardboard box that is large enough to accommodate one or two students inside it. Set the box in an open area of your classroom. Ask youngsters to help decide on the locations of the door and windows. Draw the door and windows on the box. When students are out of the classroom, use a box cutter to cut the door and window openings.

Painting the house: Place newspapers under the box to protect the floor. Then set out different colors of paint and paintbrushes. Ask one small group of children at a time to paint the outside and inside of the house. Encourage them to paint on details such as a chimney, bricks, and window sills.

Decorating the house: Provide small chairs or a beanbag for youngsters to move into the house. Ask youngsters to think of other details to add to their house, such as a toy telephone, a mailbox, or a welcome mat at the door.

Moving into the house: Add a few books to the house and then invite several youngsters at a time to settle in for a relaxing reading time.

Home, Sweet Home

©The Mailbox® • *Themes on Parade* • TEC60890

My Family

Our Family Quilt

Youngsters will feel warm and cozy after they create this fantastic family quilt! Have each student draw a picture of her family on a seven-inch square of white construction paper. Next, direct her to glue the picture to the center of a personalized nine-inch square of colored construction paper. Invite each student to decorate the resulting frame area as desired. Before piecing the quilt together, ask each child to share her quilt patch and name the family members. Mount the completed quilt patches on a length of bulletin board paper and use a marker to draw stitches around each project. Display the family quilt for all to see!

Chenille Families

These tactile chenille figures are a fun way for your little ones to showcase their families! Have each youngster count the number of family members that live in his home. Provide each student with two chenille stems for each member of his family; cut one in half. Guide students in completing the following steps to make a chenille stem person.

Step 1

Step 2

Step 3

Steps:
1. Shape half of a chenille stem into a circle to make a head; twist to hold it in place.
2. Bend the whole chenille stem in half and wrap it around the bottom of the head to make the body and legs. Bend the bottom of the legs to make feet.
3. Wrap the other half of a chenille stem around the middle of the body to make the arms.

Direct each student to repeat these steps to make the remaining family members. When finished, invite each child to share whom each figure represents. If desired, ask questions such as "Who has the largest family?" or "Who has the most sisters?" Then have students take their figures home to share with their families.

Family Concentration

This family-matching game helps youngsters see that not all families have the same members. Provide each student with a tagboard copy of the family cards on page 15. Discuss with youngsters how the families on the cards differ. Next, pair students and have each twosome mix its cards together and place them facedown in rows. In turn, each student flips over two cards. If the cards match, he keeps them. If they do not match, he turns them back over. Students continue playing in this manner until all the cards are matched. Not only are little ones learning about families, but they are practicing visual discrimination and memory skills too!

Whose Is It?

Sorting household items isn't a chore with this whole-class activity! Cut out magazine pictures that show a variety of items that different family members might use around the house, such as a crib, a swing, a hammer, a cooking pot, or a basketball. Glue each picture to a separate card and place the cards in a container. Use poster board to make a chart similar to the one shown. Post the chart on the board within students' reach. Have each youngster, in turn, remove a card from the container, state which of her family members (if any) uses the item, and tape it to the corresponding column on the chart. When all the cards are sorted, encourage students to compare how different members of their families use the items (for example, one student's father uses the cooking pot whereas another student's mother uses it). If desired, place the materials at a center so students may sort the items with a partner.

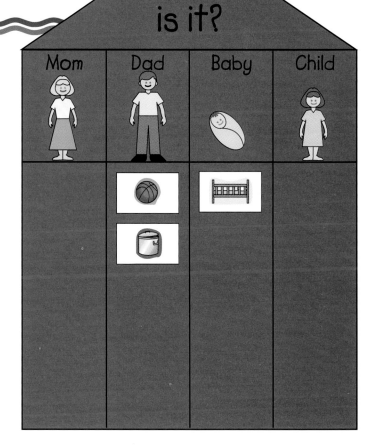

Family Names

Mama and Daddy, Nana and Papa—youngsters have an assortment of names for the members of their families! Make a chart similar to the one shown. Encourage students to share the special names they have for each family member; write their responses on the chart. Invite students to announce whether they use the same special name as another student. Next, help each student write a family member's special name on a sheet of paper and have her illustrate that person. Display these special pictures for all to see!

Nana

Mother	Father	Grandmother	Grandfather
Mom	Daddy	Nana	Papa
Mama	Dad	Granny	Pops
Mommy	Papa	Grandma	Grandpa
Momma		Mopsy	Popsy

A Family Tune

This merry tune reminds youngsters that all families have one thing in common—love!

(sung to the tune of "The Mulberry Bush")

A family is the people you love,
The people you love, the people you love.
A family is the people you love
And the people who love you!

Father, mother, sister, brother,
Grandma and grandpa, aunt and uncle—
A family is the people you love
And the people who love you!

Dramatic Play

Dress up your dramatic-play area with a variety of clothing and accessories that represent different family members and their roles! Set out items such as ties, suits, dresses, purses, briefcases, baby dolls, and children's toys. A student at this center uses the clothing and accessories to dress up as a family member. After a student is "dressed," have her tell which family member she represents. Then encourage her to use the props to act out the jobs that this family member does, such as feeding a baby or cooking dinner. No doubt little ones will gain a better understanding of their family members at this center!

Family-Style Snack

Serve up a delicious snack—family-style! You will need one bowl of a party mix snack for each group of four students. (If desired, send home a small plastic bag and a note asking each student to bring in one item to help make the party mix.) Explain that eating family-style means that all the people at the table take turns serving themselves from the same bowl. Place a bowl of party mix, a serving spoon, and napkins on each group's table. Then invite students to take turns serving themselves family-style. Remind youngsters to use good manners and wait until everyone at the table is served before eating. What a unique idea for snacktime!

Family Fun Day

Invite families to school to participate in a day of fun family festivities! Before the event, ask each family to send in a family photograph. Make two copies of it and return the original. On the day of the event, encourage family members to help their youngsters complete the following activities.

- **Fancy Frames:** Provide each family with a frame cut out of cardboard and various art supplies, such as craft foam shapes, glitter, or sequins. Have each family write "Our Family" on the top of the frame. Then invite them to decorate the frame with the materials. Give each family a copy of its photograph and have them tape it to the back of the frame. Then direct them to glue a small loop of ribbon at the top.

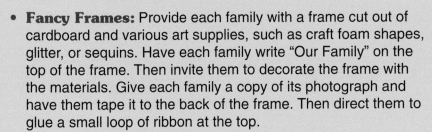

- **A Family Tree:** Draw a simple tree on a length of bulletin board paper and post it on a bulletin board or wall. Provide each family with a large apple template; access to red, green, and yellow construction paper; and the copy of their other photograph. Direct each family to trace the apple on a desired color of construction paper. Then have them cut out the pattern and glue on the photograph. Have each family attach the apple to the classroom tree.

- **Families Are Special:** Lead your little ones and their families in the following rhyme. Then serve a snack to celebrate all of their hard work!

  Families are special.
  Families are fine.
  Families are loving.
  Just look at mine!

  Families are funny.
  Families are great.
  Families are caring.
  It's time to celebrate!

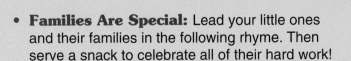

My Body

Fingers and Hands

No brushes are needed for this handy painting idea! To begin, have youngsters study their hands. Encourage them to notice the knuckles, veins, and ridges that make every set of hands unique. Next, give each youngster a sheet of white paper. Place colorful fingerpaint on the paper and prompt students to use their palms, fingertips, and even the backs of their hands to make a unique painting. That's a whole lot of creativity right at your youngsters' fingertips!

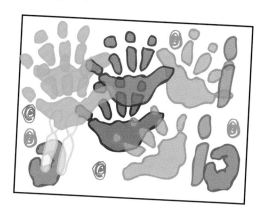

Self-Portraits

Mirror, mirror, I can see that I am as special as can be! With this nifty idea, youngsters use mirrors to help make detailed self-portraits. Gather a small group of students and give each child a mirror. Encourage each youngster to study himself in the mirror, prompting him to notice specific details about his reflection, such as the color of his eyes, the shape of his nose, and the length of his eyelashes. Next, give each student a large piece of drawing paper. Invite him to draw a self-portrait, checking his reflection to ensure accuracy. Mount the finished portraits on colorful paper. Then attach them to a bulletin board around an aluminum foil mirror. Under the mirror write the text shown. What an eye-catching display!

Mirror, mirror, I can see
That I am as special as can be!

Growing Up

With this fun sequencing center, students place pictures of people in chronological order! Gather a magazine picture of a person for each of the following life stages: baby, toddler, child, teenager, young adult, older adult, and senior citizen. Mount the pictures on tagboard and laminate them for durability. Then place the pictures at a center. Invite a youngster to the center and encourage him to sequence the pictures in a row from baby to senior citizen. For a challenge, invite each student to name each stage, as mentioned above.

In the Spotlight!

Youngsters spotlight different parts of the body with this brilliant idea! Enlarge a copy of the body pattern on page 21. Then post it in your large-group area. Dim the lights. Give a child a small flashlight and encourage him to point the beam of light toward the pattern and illuminate an elbow. When the child correctly spotlights an elbow, invite the remaining students to point to one of their own elbows. Continue in the same way, asking different children to highlight other body parts on the pattern.

Self-Care Tools

What do a hairbrush, dental floss, and a washcloth have in common? They're all self-care tools! Build excitement about self-care tools with this mystery bag activity! Place each of the following items in a bag: a hairbrush, a comb, a toothbrush, a facial tissue, a washcloth, and a bar of soap. Without allowing the children to see inside the bag, encourage a youngster to reach in and pull out an item. Invite the student and her classmates to explain what the self-care tool is used for and why it is important. Repeat the process for each remaining item. That's quite a self-care collection!

This Is My Body

Youngsters highlight ways to take care of their bodies with this fun action song! Lead students in singing the song, encouraging them to act out the final line. Next, invite a student to suggest a different way he can take care of his body. Then repeat the song, replacing the last line with the child's suggestion. Continue in the same way for several verses.

(sung to the tune of "The Wheels on the Bus")

This is my body; I take care of it,
Take care of it, take care of it.
This is my body; I take care of it
[By brushing my teeth.]

Dramatic Play

Add some zing to dramatic-play time with this accessory sort! Label each of several containers with a picture of a different body part as shown. Place the containers in your dramatic-play area. Invite students to dress up and play. After youngsters are finished using the dramatic-play center, encourage them to sort the dress-up items according to their corresponding body parts. For example, earmuffs go in the ear container, sunglasses go in the eye container, and shoes go in the foot container.

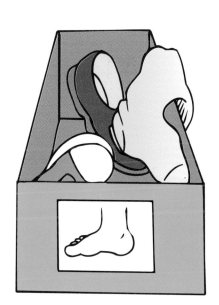

Cookie Snack

These cookie kids are a tasty treat! For each child, make or purchase a gingerbread person or a person-shaped sugar cookie. Have each youngster spread frosting on her cookie. Then invite her to add features with M&M's Minis candies and chocolate chips. Finally, invite youngsters to eat their cookie kids. Mmm, mmm!

Wrapping It Up

Five Senses Day

Explore the five senses with special activities devoted to hearing, seeing, touching, tasting, and smelling.

Hearing: Set out three identical boxes. Place an item that makes noise, such as a softly playing tape recorder in one box. Then place a lid on each box. Encourage students to identify which box the noise is coming from. After they correctly identify the box, prompt students to close their eyes. Then mix up the boxes and play another round.

Seeing: Place several natural items at a table, such as seashells, pinecones, rocks, leaves, and sticks. Also place several nonbreakable magnifying glasses at the table. Encourage students to observe the items with their eyes. Then invite them to look at the objects through a magnifying glass, prompting them to notice how the magnifying glass makes small details clearly visible.

Touching: Collect several items that can easily be identified by touch, such as a toy car, a marker, a block, and a ball. Place each item in a sock and then tie a knot in the end of the sock. Invite youngsters to feel each sock and identify the item.

Smelling: Place several nonbreakable vases at a table, and place a different flower in each one. (Be sure to choose flowers that have distinctive smells.) Place glue, a class supply of flower cutouts, and a graph similar to the one shown near the flowers. Invite each student to smell the flowers and choose his favorite; then help him write his name on a cutout and glue it next to the corresponding flower on the graph.

Tasting: Provide a variety of sweet foods and sour foods, such as cookies, strawberry slices, dill pickle slices and lemon slices. Invite students to try a small sample of each kind of food. Encourage them to describe the taste of each food. Then prompt them to identify which foods are sweet and which are sour.

Flower Favorites

🌼	Josh	Eli	Anna
🌼	Ashley	Nick	
🌷	John		

Nutrition

Fruit Trees

Plant the seed of healthy snacking as youngsters create this fresh fruit tree. Talk about fruits with your youngsters, leading them to conclude that fruits are good to eat as well as good for the body. Next, have them think about where fruits grow. Explain that some fruits grow on trees and give examples, such as lemons, oranges, apples, cherries, pears, and plums. Then invite each child to make a fruit tree. Give each child a copy of page 27 and have him color the leaves green and the trunk brown. Then provide access to shallow pans of washable tempera paint in fruit colors. Encourage him to choose one type of fruit and then press his finger into the appropriate color of paint and make several fingerprints to represent that fruit growing on his tree. If desired, follow with a tasting party of fruits that grow on trees. Delicious!

Fruits and Vegetables

Crafting these mouthwatering fruit and veggie models is sure to intrigue your little ones! Use the recipe shown to make enough play clay for your group. Give each child a portion of clay and encourage her to shape it into her favorite fruit or vegetable. Help her insert a paper clip into the end of her creation to form a hanger; then set it aside to dry on a cooling rack. Let the creations air-dry for several days and then invite students to paint them with tempera paint. When the paint is dry, spray each creation with acrylic sealer, if desired. Help each child tie a ribbon hanger on her fruit or vegetable to make an ornament. Then invite each child to take it home to display in the kitchen as a reminder to eat healthy fruits and vegetables!

Play Clay
(makes enough for six children)

1 c. cornstarch
2 c. baking soda
1¼ c. water

Combine the ingredients in a microwave-safe bowl. Stir well. Heat in the microwave for four minutes, stirring at 30 second intervals. The mixture will thicken to the consistency of mashed potatoes. (Or the mixture can be cooked in a saucepan on the stovetop over low heat until it has thickened—about 15 minutes.) Spread the clay on a baking sheet and let it sit until cool enough to handle. Knead until smooth. Store the clay in resealable plastic bags in the refrigerator.

Rainbow of Foods

Eating a rainbow of foods is nutritious, so give youngsters a chance to plan pretend meals with this colorful activity! In advance, cut out magazine pictures of healthy foods in a variety of colors, such as red strawberries, white milk, orange cheese, yellow bananas, green broccoli, brown rice, purple eggplant, and so forth. Find several pictures of foods in each color. Mount each picture onto a tagboard card and laminate the pictures for durability, if desired. Gather students; then arrange three or four foods of the same color on a large paper plate. Have students look at the plate and decide whether the foods make a healthy meal. Lead students to conclude that the meal would be better if there were more colors on the plate. Then have a volunteer choose foods that would make a healthier meal. Encourage each child to take a turn planning a nutritious, colorful meal using the foods provided. "Delish"!

Musical Chairs

Try this variation on the traditional musical chairs game to build more awareness of healthy food groups. Arrange two rows of chairs back-to-back, making sure there is a chair for each child. Using the food cards made in "Rainbow of Foods," above, tape one card to each chair. Discuss the basic food groups with children and then have them stand around the chairs. Play some lively music and have children march around the chairs. Stop the music and invite each child to sit in the nearest chair. Then call out a food group and encourage all the children sitting on pictures of foods in that group to stand up. If desired, ask each child standing to name her food. Play more rounds in this manner until each food group has been named. Now that's a great way to learn about food groups!

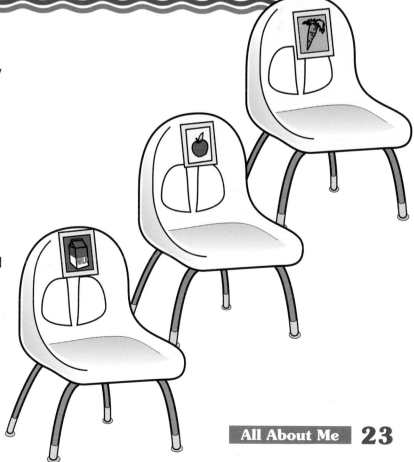

Class Cookbook

Beef up little ones' understanding of nutritious foods by creating a cookbook that will be a treasured family keepsake! Ask each child's family to send in a favorite nutritious recipe. Have a parent volunteer type each recipe on a separate sheet of paper. Encourage each child to illustrate his recipe with a picture of the dish drawn in black fine-tip marker. Copy each page to make a class supply. Program a cover with the title "Our Favorite Healthy Recipes" and then copy it onto construction paper for each child. Then stack a set of pages behind a cover to make a book for each child. Bind each book by stapling it along the left side. Invite each youngster to decorate his cookbook cover and then take his copy home to share with his family.

To Stay Healthy

(sung to the tune of "Mary Had a Little Lamb")

Eat your fruits and vegetables,
Vegetables, vegetables.
Eat your fruits and vegetables
To stay healthy.

Eat your protein and your bread,
And your bread, and your bread.
Eat your protein and your bread
To stay healthy.

Drink your milk, three cups a day,
Three cups a day, three cups a day.
Drink your milk, three cups a day,
To stay healthy.

Dramatic Play

Serve up nutrition knowledge as youngsters pretend to make a meal. Stock your dramatic-play center with healthy play foods and empty, clean containers from real foods. Also include aprons, cookbooks, plastic plates, and grocery store ads. Encourage students in this center to take turns preparing, serving, and eating healthy meals, making sure each plateful is colorful. Supper's ready!

Yummy Dough

Squish it. Sculpt it. Eat it? When the play dough is based with nutritious peanut butter, playtime doubles as snacktime! (If you have a student with peanut allergies, substitute soy nut butter for the peanut butter.) Give each child a small bowl containing one tablespoon of peanut butter, one tablespoon of toasted wheat germ, one teaspoon of powdered nonfat milk, and one teaspoon of honey. Invite her to mix the ingredients with her hands, kneading it well. (You may wish to provide a paper plate or sheet of waxed paper to make a clean work surface for kneading and sculpting the dough.) When youngsters have had time to play with their dough, serve cups of cold milk and invite them to eat their protein-rich play dough for a snack.

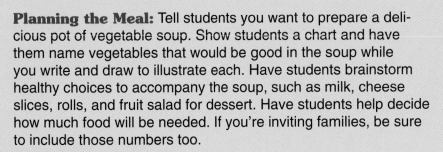

Cooking Up Nutritious Fun

Get your youngsters involved in planning and preparing a nutritious meal, and they're sure to enjoy eating it even more! Plan a day to cook with your class and then enjoy the resulting meal together. You may even wish to invite families to join in on the fun!

Planning the Meal: Tell students you want to prepare a delicious pot of vegetable soup. Show students a chart and have them name vegetables that would be good in the soup while you write and draw to illustrate each. Have students brainstorm healthy choices to accompany the soup, such as milk, cheese slices, rolls, and fruit salad for dessert. Have students help decide how much food will be needed. If you're inviting families, be sure to include those numbers too.

Making the List: Using the chart made above, enlist student help to write a shopping list for the items you will need to buy for the meal. Also consult the chart to decide how much of each food will be needed. Have students help you write notes home to request different types of vegetables for the soup. If you're inviting families, send home invitations with the needed information. Recruit adult helpers for the cooking day.

Cooking Day: Bring the groceries to school and enlist student help in unpacking each item. Have a student find each item and mark it off the shopping list to ensure all the needed supplies were purchased. Divide students into small groups, each with an adult helper. Give each group a task, such as washing vegetables, peeling vegetables, opening cans, measuring chopped veggies into the pot, stirring the soup, and so forth, depending on age and ability. While waiting for the soup to cook, have each child make a placemat by drawing pictures of nutritious foods on a sheet of construction paper. Have each student set her place at the table with her placemat, a plastic spoon, napkins, and a drink. When the soup is ready, serve each child (and guest) a bowlful with any sides that your students helped prepare.

Enjoying the Meal: It's time to sit back with a hot bowl of nourishing soup! Invite students to talk with guests about the healthy foods they're enjoying for lunch.

My Community

"Wheel-y" Painting

Roll right through an introduction of community helpers with toy vehicles and this painting idea. To prepare, pour several colors of paint into separate shallow pans. Then gather a supply of toy vehicles used by community helpers, such as a police car, a fire engine, a tow truck, an ambulance, a bus, and a garbage truck. Introduce each vehicle to students and talk about the corresponding community helper's job. Then give each child in a small group a white sheet of construction paper. Have each youngster choose a vehicle, dip its wheels in paint, and then roll it across his paper to create tracks. Encourage him to choose several different vehicles and colors of paint to make tracks. When the paint is dry, have him share his painting with the group and tell about one community helper vehicle he used to complete his project. Honk, honk! Fire truck coming through!

Hats Off to You

Students' drawings complete the uniforms for these community helpers. In advance, cut out magazine pictures of community helpers who typically wear hats, such as construction workers, mail carriers, police officers, firefighters, and bakers or chefs. Carefully cut off the hat of each community helper and discard it. Glue each cutout on a sheet of paper. After the glue has dried, give each child a prepared paper. Have her think about the type of hat the helper would wear. Then instruct her to draw a hat to complete the picture. Invite her to share her picture with the group. Then bind all the pages along with a cover titled "Hats Off to Community Helpers."

City Maps

No learner's permit is needed for this activity, which has youngsters practicing beginning map skills! To prepare, make a class set of the map on page 33. Give each child a copy and have her color the buildings and other features on her map as she desires. Then have each child use a black marker to draw streets on her map. After the maps are complete, provide each child with a toy vehicle and have her follow your directions as she drives her vehicle on the map. Give suggestions such as "Drive from the park to the school" or "Drive from the hospital to the police station." Now that's some good driving!

Tools of the Trade

This guessing game will have little ones learning about various community helpers and the tools they use. Gather a collection of tools used by several community helpers. For example, you might obtain a hard hat (construction worker), a whistle (police officer), a whisk (chef or baker), a piece of chalk (teacher), and a stethoscope (doctor). To begin, seat students in a circle. Hold up each tool, in turn, and lead a discussion about who uses the tool and how it's used. Then pass each tool around the circle so students can have a closer look. Cool tools!

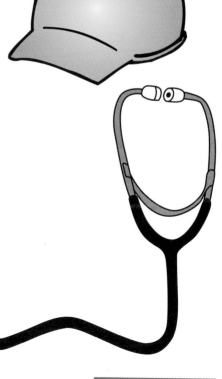

A Sign Book

Little ones will be eager to read this book over and over—all by themselves! To prepare, photograph various signs in your community, such as traffic signs, safety signs, and signs for well-known stores and restaurants. Place the developed photos in a photo album. Share the resulting book with students and use the photos to talk about the various signs found in the community. Then place the book in your reading area and encourage youngsters to read it to each other. Hey, I know that sign!

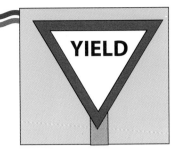

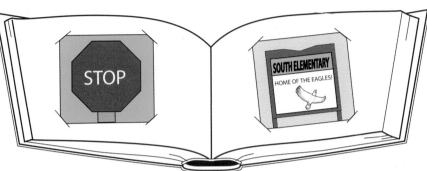

My Community

Youngsters get acquainted with the various aspects of their community with this catchy song.

(sung to the tune of "Twinkle, Twinkle, Little Star")

In my community you will find
Helpers of most every kind—
Firefighters, doctors, teachers, too,
Police officers and vets at the zoo.
In my community you will find
Helpers of most every kind.

In my community you will find
Buildings of most every kind—
Tall ones, short ones, long ones, too,
High ones, low ones, and houses too.
In my community you will find
Buildings of most every kind.

In my community you will find
People of most every kind.
Happy, sad, and grumpy, too,
Laughing, singing, smiling at you.
In my community you will find
People of most every kind.

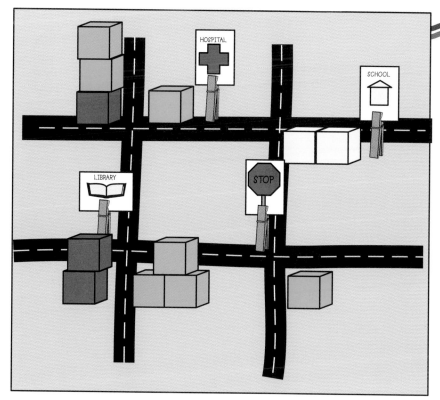

Dramatic Play

A city model takes shape—complete with signs—when you use this dramatic-play idea. To prepare, cut index cards in half; then draw a different sign on each card, such as signs for traffic or safety, a school, a library, a park, a fire station, a hospital, and restaurants. Clip a spring-type clothespin to each sign and then show youngsters how to stand the sign. Place the signs in your block area and encourage students to build buildings. Then have them use the signs to label the buildings and the streets. Be sure to have on hand extra cards, markers, and clothespins for students to use to make additional signs.

A Baker's Snack

This yummy snack is easy to make and fun to eat! Discuss with youngsters a baker's job and talk about how he might use a rolling pin to roll out dough. Explain to little ones that they will be using a rolling pin for this snack. Have each child in a small group wash her hands. Then give her a paper plate and a slice of bread. Ask her to pretend to be a baker as she uses a rolling pin to flatten the bread. Next, instruct her to use a plastic knife to spread a thin layer of jam on the bread. Then have her carefully roll the bread as shown. Invite each little baker to enjoy her rolled up snack. Yum!

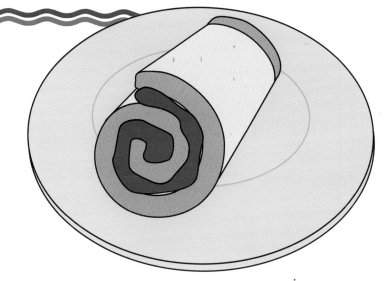

Build a Community

When youngsters' ideas about community merge, the results are great! Get your little engineers involved in creating and building a community all their own.

The City Limits: Lay sheets of newspaper on the floor. Spread a white flat sheet on the paper. Have each child put on a smock and then paint roads, rivers, and other features on the sheet to create a map. Allow the paint to dry.

Time to Build: Lead students to discuss the types of buildings found in a community. List the buildings on a chart and add a picture clue for easy student reference. Provide students with a collection of various empty, clean boxes and containers, such as food boxes, yogurt containers, small soda bottles, and cylindrical oatmeal containers. Give students access to markers, construction paper, and glue. Have students use the supplies to make the buildings listed on the chart.

Block Party: Have students position their buildings on the map they created. Lead youngsters to discuss how people would get from building to building. Are more roads or bridges needed? If so, use a permanent marker to add more roads.

Community Time: Have students decide on a name for the community. Then help them make a sign welcoming guests to the community. Have students take turns giving tours and pointing out the buildings and important features of the community.

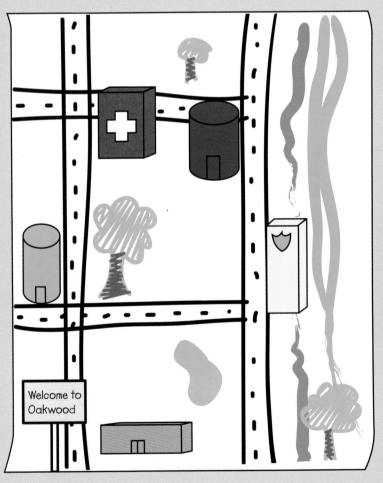

Welcome to Oakwood

SCHOOL

PARK

HOSPITAL

LIBRARY

BOOKS

SUPERMARKET

POLICE STATION

POLICE

Note to the teacher: Use with "City Maps" on page 29.

All About Me Parade

Plan an All About Me Parade with youngsters. Divide students into five groups; then assign each group a different topic from the list below. Use the ideas given for each topic to make costumes and props. Then teach youngsters the song on page 35 and let the parade begin!

Homes: Have students draw and color different types of homes on a strip of bulletin board paper to make a banner. Have several students carry the banner to lead the parade. Invite other students to carry their art projects from "Build a Home" on page 4.

Family: Ask several children to dress up like different family members and carry baby dolls. Have some youngsters carry their projects from "Chenille Family" on page 10. Invite other students to carry photographs of their families.

Healthy Body: Invite a child to wear a skeleton sweatshirt. (To make one, attach masking tape in a bone pattern on a black sweatshirt.) Have the remaining students carry personal care items such as toothbrushes and combs. Encourage students to show off their strong muscles as they parade.

Nutrition: Have each child wear a healthy foods crown. (To make a crown, have each youngster attach a variety of stickers of healthy foods onto a personalized headband.) Ask several students to carry their projects from "Fruit Trees" on page 22. Have other students carry real or plastic fruits and vegetables.

Community: Have some students wear community helper hats. Invite several students to carry toy vehicles such as fire trucks and police cars. Ask other students to carry their maps from "City Maps" on page 29.

All About Me Parade Song

(sung to the tune of "When Johnny Comes Marching Home")

The children are marching into town. Hooray! Hooray!
The children are marching in an All About Me parade!
First come children with homes big and small.
There are so many we can't count them all.
Oh, we're so glad the children could come today.

The children are marching into town. Hooray! Hooray!
The children are marching in an All About Me parade.
Next come families of every size.
Your family loves you—that's no surprise.
Oh, we're so glad the children could come today.

The children are marching into town. Hooray! Hooray!
The children are marching in an All About Me parade.
Then come children with health on their mind.
They want to stay healthy—they really shine.
Oh, we're so glad the children could come today.

The children are marching into town. Hooray! Hooray!
The children are marching in an All About Me parade.
Here come children with healthy food.
They are in a really great mood.
Oh, we're so glad the children could come today.

The children are marching into town. Hooray! Hooray!
The children are marching in an All About Me parade.
Last come children who want to say,
"The community is where we live and play."
Oh, we're so glad the children could come today.

Farm

Barn Buddies

Your little farmers are sure to share their knowledge of farm animals when they do this art activity. For each child, fold a 4½" x 12" strip of red construction paper to make barn doors as shown. Also cut out a construction paper roof shape for each child. Use a permanent marker to add details to the barn doors and roof. Set out farm animal stickers or rubber stamps and stamp pads with washable ink. To begin, ask youngsters to name farm animals. Then give each child a barn and help him glue on the roof. Help him open the barn doors and then attach stickers or use stamps to fill his barn with farm animals. If desired, display the projects on a bulletin board with a silo, a pond, and other farm-related cutouts.

Hey, Scarecrow!

Bring smiles to youngsters' faces with this happy scarecrow puppet. For each child, cut out a construction paper copy of the scarecrow patterns on page 41. Give each student a set of patterns and a 9" x 12" sheet of poster board. Have her draw a face on the head and then color the patterns. Next, have her glue the patterns onto the poster board to make a scarecrow. Then help her glue pieces of yellow yarn or raffia under the edges of the pants, shirt, and neck to complete the scarecrow as shown. After the glue is dry, cut around the scarecrow and attach it to a large craft stick to make a puppet for each child. Invite youngsters to use their puppets for a scarecrow parade around the classroom.

Who's Got the Egg?

Cluck, cluck, cluck! This small-group guessing game is "eggs-tra" fun! Cut out three colored construction paper copies of the hen pattern on page 42 and attach each one to an upside down paper cup. Place the cups on a table in front of your group. Put a cotton ball egg under one cup as youngsters observe. Next, slowly rearrange the cups without lifting them off the table. Then ask the group to guess which hen is hiding the egg. After the egg is found, repeat the activity until each child has had a turn to guess.

Where in the Barn?

Encourage your little farmers to practice following directions with this flannelboard activity. Copy, color, cut out, and laminate the farm animal patterns on pages 42 and 43 and then prepare them for flannelboard use. Also, cut three simple barn shapes from red felt. Place each barn on your flannelboard and lay the animal cutouts nearby. Gather students and ask one child to follow directions such as "Place a pig on the first barn, a hen on the last barn, and a sheep on the middle barn." After verifying the youngster's work, repeat the activity with additional students and new directions.

Farm Story

This whole-group activity creates a farm story that's sure to be an original. Gather several different plastic farm animals and place them in a paper bag. Sit in a circle with youngsters and begin telling them a made-up farm story. Next, draw one animal from the bag and incorporate it into your story. Pass the bag to a child and have him draw one animal from the bag and say its name. Then continue the story, including the chosen animal. Repeat this process until all of the animals have been removed from the bag. As a variation, ask each child to contribute to the farm story after he has pulled an animal from the bag.

On the Farm

Fill your classroom with farm sounds as youngsters sing this lively tune. Gather the animal cutouts from "Where in the Barn?" on page 37 and a flannelboard to prompt youngsters as they sing. Place the hen on the flannelboard and lead youngsters in singing the following verse. Then continue by singing it four more times, each time replacing the animal name and sound and changing the animal cutout.

(sung to the tune "The Wheels on the Bus")

If you see a [hen], go [cluck, cluck, cluck],
[Cluck, cluck, cluck, cluck, cluck, cluck].
If you see a [hen], go [cluck, cluck, cluck]
Down on the farm.

pig, oink
cow, moo
sheep, baa
horse, neigh

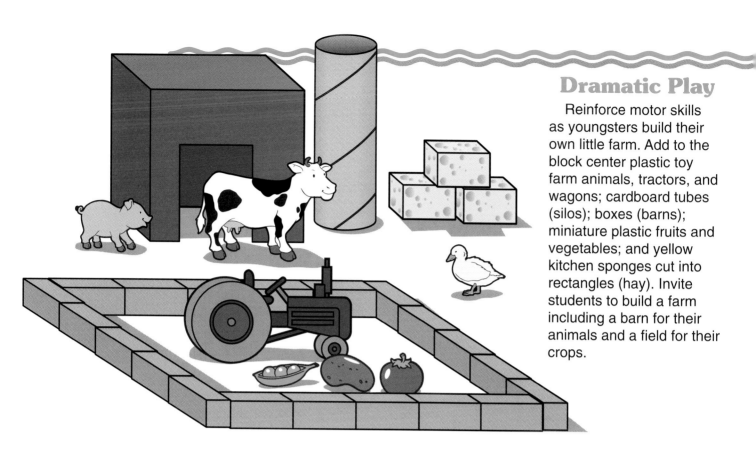

Dramatic Play

Reinforce motor skills as youngsters build their own little farm. Add to the block center plastic toy farm animals, tractors, and wagons; cardboard tubes (silos); boxes (barns); miniature plastic fruits and vegetables; and yellow kitchen sponges cut into rectangles (hay). Invite students to build a farm including a barn for their animals and a field for their crops.

Sloppy Snack

Here, piggy, piggy! Be prepared for squeals of delight when youngsters dig into this sloppy snack. For each child, place a scoop of pudding in a clear plastic cup to represent a pig trough. Set out bowls of cereal, mini chocolate chips, M&M's Minis candies, and sprinkles to represent leftover food. Explain to youngsters that some farm pigs are fed leftover food that is mixed together and put in a trough. Tell them the mixture is called slop. Then give each child a trough and a plastic spoon (shovel). Invite each student to shovel a scoop of each leftover into his trough and mix it together to make slop. Then dig in!

Wrapping It Up

Down on Our Farm

Your little farmers will enjoy creating props and performing this sing-along farm animal puppet show.

Farm Animal Puppets: Give each child a white construction paper cutout of one farm animal from page 42 or 43. Have her color her animal. Then tape each animal cutout onto a craft stick to make a puppet.

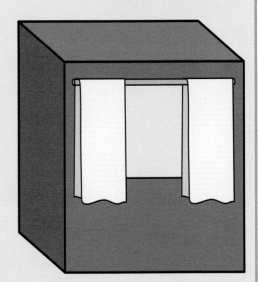

Puppet Stage: Locate a large cardboard box and cut a window from one side of it. Invite youngsters to paint it to resemble a barn. Make a curtain by cutting a pillowcase in half to make two panels. Then lay the panels over a dowel and attach the dowel to the stage.

Invitations: Program your puppet show date and time on a sheet of paper and then make a copy for each child. Also cut out a red construction paper barn shape for each child. Trim the invitation and mount it onto the barn cutout to make a card. Then have each youngster take one card home to invite his parents to the show.

The Puppet Show Song: Teach youngsters the song below. Model how to go behind the stage and perform the song with a puppet. Divide youngsters into groups by type of animal puppet. Next, have one group at a time practice performing with its puppets as the class sings the corresponding verse. Then invite parents or another class to a fun performance.

(sung to the tune of "Frére Jacques")

See the [pigs], see the [pigs]
In their [pens], in their [pens].
Hear them as they [oink].
Hear them as they [oink].
[Oink, oink, oink].
[Oink, oink, oink].

cows, barn, moo
horses, field, neigh
sheep, meadow, baa
hens, coop, cluck

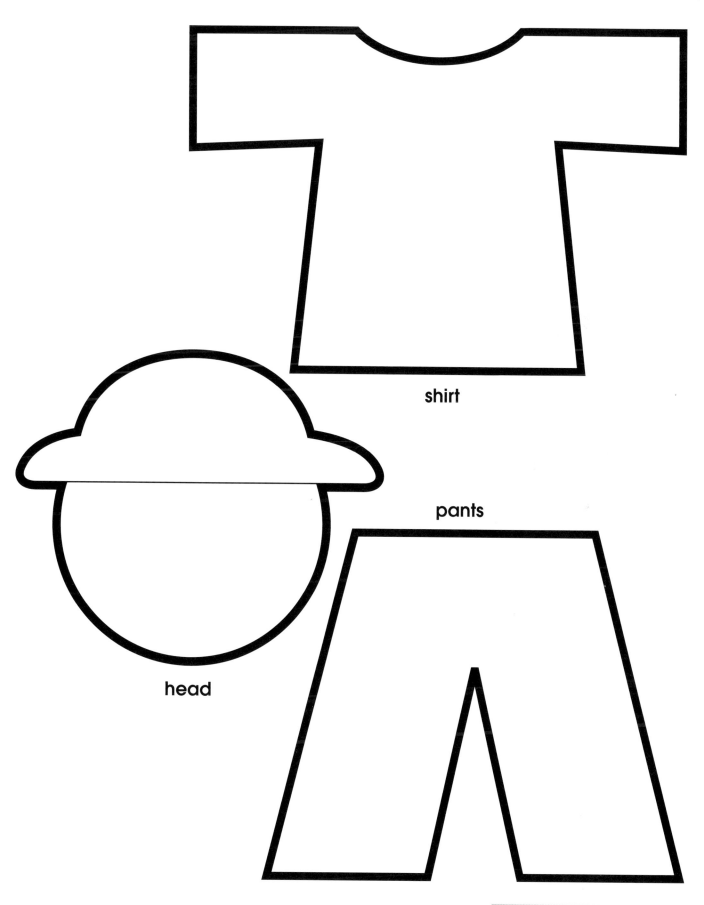

shirt

pants

head

Farm Animal Patterns

Use with "Who's Got the Egg?" and "Where in the Barn?" on page 37 and "Farm Animal Puppets" on page 40.

Ocean

Ocean Scenes

These pretty underwater scenes are just right for getting youngsters interested in oceans! Give each child a sheet of white drawing paper and crayons. Have him draw an underwater scene that includes fish, sand, seaweed, and other ocean life. Encourage him to color his picture, making sure to press down hard on the crayons. Then have him paint over his entire picture with water-thinned blue tempera paint. When the paint is dry, display the ocean scenes for all to admire.

Paper Plate Fish

Your little ones will enjoy making a school of colorful fish! Give each child a paper plate. Also give her a plate that has been cut in three sections as shown. Help her tape the plate half to the whole plate to form a tail. Then help her tape the plate quarters to resemble fins as shown. Next, invite her to color her fish as desired. Have her complete her fish by adding a round sticker eye. If desired, suspend each fish from the ceiling to give an underwater feel to your classroom. It's an ocean in here!

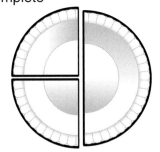

Ocean Puzzles

Puzzling over a fun activity for your little ones? Try this! Cut out full-page magazine pictures of ocean life. Glue each picture to a different sheet of tagboard. Laminate the pictures for durability if desired. Then puzzle-cut each picture into three or four pieces. Store each puzzle in a different envelope and place them in a center. Invite each child to take a turn assembling each puzzle.

Dolphin Moves

Invite youngsters to dive into some dramatic play when you share some dolphin training tips with them. Dolphins can be trained to do tricks that entertain people. Explain that trainers teach dolphins to do tricks with hand motions and whistle blows. When the dolphin does the trick, it is rewarded. Then encourage each child to follow your directions as he pretends to be a dolphin. (See the list of suggested directions and accompanying hand motions.) Reward each child for his hard work with nothing other than a handful of fish-shaped crackers!

Direction	Hand Motion
Turn around.	*Rotate index finger.*
Swim around the room.	*Roll hands.*
Pretend to dive.	*Point down.*
Jump.	*Clap once.*

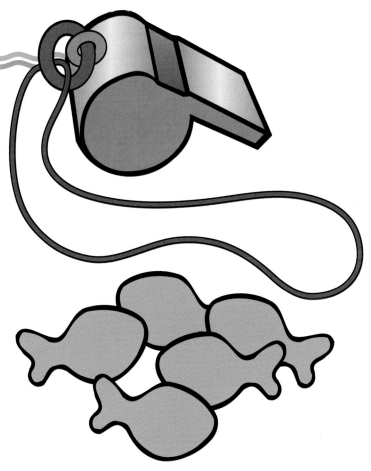

Fishing With Friends

Let's go fishing and see what letter pairs we catch! Duplicate the fish cards on page 49 to make a class supply. Program each pair with a different lowercase letter and then cut apart the cards. Laminate them for durability if desired. Give each child one card and have her study it carefully. Then, on your signal, encourage students to walk around the room searching for the child with the matching fish. When each twosome has paired up, ask them to try to identify their letter and decide if either child has it in her name. Go fish!

In the Deep Blue Sea

Use this little ditty to introduce youngsters to just a few critters who call the ocean their home!

(sung to the tune of "Old MacDonald Had a Farm")

There are crabs both big and small
In the deep blue sea.
There are crabs; look for them all
In the deep blue sea.
With a pinch, pinch here and a pinch, pinch there.
Here a pinch, there a pinch, everywhere a pinch, pinch.
There are crabs both big and small
In the deep blue sea.

There are fish both big and small
In the deep blue sea.
There are fish; look for them all
In the deep blue sea.
With a splish, splash here and a splish, splash there.
Here a splish, there a splash, everywhere a splish, splash.
There are fish both big and small
In the deep blue sea.

There are sharks both big and small
In the deep blue sea.
There are sharks; look for them all
In the deep blue sea.
With a chomp, chomp here and a chomp, chomp there.
Here a chomp, there a chomp, everywhere a chomp, chomp.
There are sharks both big and small
In the deep blue sea.

Dramatic Play

"Meet me under the sea!" You're sure to hear similar exclamations when you set up this seaworthy dramatic-play center. Show students pictures of ocean scenes. Include plenty of interesting ocean life such as fish, shells, plants, and coral. Then place a blue sheet on the floor and encourage youngsters to use blocks, plastic fish, large seashells, and artificial aquarium plants to create their own ocean scenes.

Seaweed Snack

Serve up this seaworthy snack! In advance, cut rolled green Fruit Roll-Ups fruit snacks into a class supply of quarter-inch slices. (One fruit snack provides approximately eight slices.) Tint a tub of whipped topping blue to resemble ocean water. Give each child a graham cracker, a slice of the fruit snack, a few fish-shaped crackers, a paper plate, and access to the whipped topping and a plastic knife. Invite her to spread the whipped topping on the cracker. Next, have her unroll her fruit snack and tear it into several pieces. Have her place the pieces on top of the whipped topping to resemble seaweed. Then have her add the fish-shaped crackers to complete her seaweed snack!

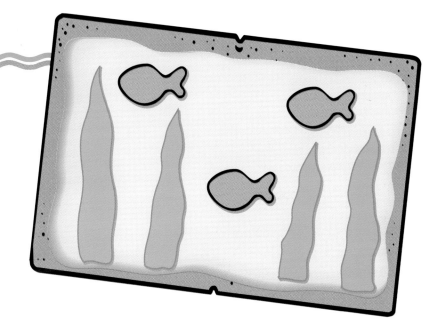

Wrapping It Up

Tide Pool Mural

Look what the tide brought in—this beautiful, briny mural featuring your youngsters' artwork! Explain to students that the place where the ocean and the land meet and overlap is called the intertidal zone. Then use the ideas below to make a cooperative mural.

Tide Pools: To begin the mural, hang a length of tan bulletin board paper on a wall at childrens' eye level. Enlist student help to cut several large tide pool shapes from blue bulletin board paper. Have them glue the tide pools onto the tan paper. If desired, have children cut rock shapes from gray paper and glue them to the mural.

Sea Stars: Cut star shapes from construction paper. Let children color the stars as desired. Then invite each child to add dots to each of the legs with a glitter glue pen to resemble the spiny bumps. Then glue or tape the sea stars to the mural.

Hermit Crabs: Purchase or find a variety of shells, especially hermit crab shells. Use a hot glue gun to attach each shell to the mural. Have youngsters draw a hermit crab head and pincers coming out of appropriate shells.

Anemones: Cut a three-inch oval for each anemone. Cut chenille stems into thirds. Invite a child to bend several chenille pieces in half and then tape each to an oval to form a three-dimensional anemone. Tape or glue the completed anemones to the mural.

Fish: Gather a class supply of new wooden ice-cream spoons. Have each child paint a spoon with gray tempera. While the paint is wet, help him shake on silver glitter. When the paint is dry, have him shake off the excess glitter and add a white hole reinforcer for an eye. Glue or tape the fish to the mural.

Pond

Water Lilies

Leapin' lily pads! Youngsters strengthen their fine-motor skills as they create these pretty pond flowers! Set out shallow bowls of glue on a newspaper-covered area. Give each child a large green lily pad shape and a supply of three-inch pink tissue paper squares. Model for students how to crumple a piece of tissue paper, dip it in glue, and stick it onto a lily pad. Have each child copy this process to make flowers on her lily pad as shown. If desired, display the water lilies along the border of a bulletin board.

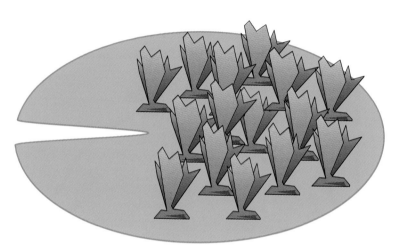

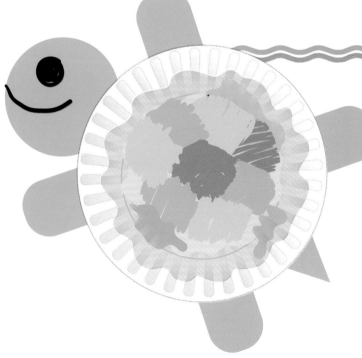

Painted Turtles

Unique shell designs pop up when youngsters use this paint wash method. Set out several different shades of green crayons and a shallow dish of water-thinned green paint. Show youngsters several different pictures of turtles and discuss the design on each shell. Then have each child create his own uniquely designed turtle. Have each student use the green crayons to draw and color a design on a white paper plate to make a turtle shell. Then help him brush the green paint over his turtle shell. When the paint is dry, have each child cut out legs, a tail, and a head from construction paper and glue the parts onto his shell to complete his turtle.

Matching Mothers and Babies

"Pond-ering" how to teach youngsters which animals live in and around a pond? Try this matching game. Make a tagboard copy of the animal cards on page 55. Then color the cards, cut them out, and laminate them for durability. If possible, show students pictures of animals that live in and around a pond, including fish, turtles, bullfrogs, herons, and raccoons. Then invite a pair of students to mix up the cards and work together to match each mother with her baby.

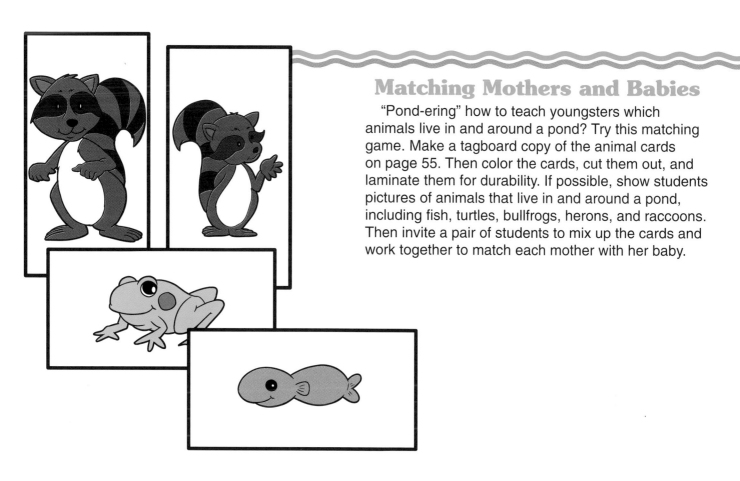

Catch the Fly

Ribbit, ribbit! Pretending to be a frog makes this game hoppin' fun! Have youngsters sit in a circle and ask them to pretend to be frogs resting around a pond. Show them a beach ball and ask them to pretend that it is a fly, which frogs eat. Next, toss the fly up and quickly call out the name of one child. Have her hop up and catch the fly. Then have her gently toss the fly and call out a different child's name. Have the first child return to her spot by the pond as the other child catches the fly. Continue in the same manner until each little frog has had a turn catching the fly.

Down at the Pond

This pond full of constructive beavers will help build up youngsters' language skills. Have a small group of youngsters sit in a circle, and invite one child to stand in the center. Ask the standing child to pretend to be a beaver building a dam as you read the first verse of the following rhyme aloud. At the end of the first verse, have the little beaver call on a classmate to join him in the center to help build. Then read the second verse of the rhyme and have the second child call someone to the center. Encourage youngsters to repeat the second verse, updating the number word each time until each little beaver is busy building.

One little beaver in the beaver pond,
Building a dam from dusk to dawn.
He calls a friend to help him out.

Now there are [two] little beavers in the beaver pond
Building a dam from dusk to dawn.
They call a friend to help them out.

Full of Life

Use this lively tune to introduce youngsters to pond life.

(sung to the tune of "Three Blind Mice")

Full of life.
Full of life.
Water, land, and air.
Water, land, and air.
The pond is a busy place to go,
With frogs, insects, and little minnows.
Beavers can make their own ponds, you know.
Full of life.
Full of life.

Dramatic Play

Promote cooperative learning as youngsters work together at this beaver pond. Use a round blue tablecloth or cut a pond shape from a blue plastic shower curtain and lay it flat on the floor. Randomly place a few round green pillows in the pond to represent lily pads. If desired, place artificial plants in and around the pond area. Next, place a tub of cylindrical blocks (logs) and a few toy beavers or stuffed animals near the pond. Show students pictures of a beaver dam. Tell youngsters that a portion of the beaver dam can be seen above water, but some of it is underwater. Then invite several students to pretend to be beavers as they build a dam in the pond.

Pond Snack

This little blue pond promotes healthy snacking! Tint a container of lowfat ranch dip blue and gather fish-shaped crackers and cucumber slices. Cut a V-shaped notch from each cucumber slice to make a lily pad as shown. Give each child a paper plate with a tablespoon of dip on it. Have her swirl the dip around with her finger to make a pond. Next, give each child several fish and lily pads to add to her pond. Then invite each child to go fishing for her tasty treat.

Wrapping It Up

Pond, Sweet Pond

Conclude your pond unit by having youngsters use the following ideas to make a pond display.

The Pond: Mount brown bulletin board paper on a wall to represent mud around the pond. Cut a pond shape from shiny blue foil wrapping paper or blue bulletin board paper and attach it to the center of the mud.

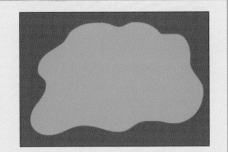

Beaver Dam: Have students crumble brown paper bags to represent twigs and then glue them onto one section of the pond to make a beaver dam.

Pond Plants: Attach several lily pads from "Water Lilies" (page 50) to the pond. Have several students tear construction paper cattails or grass and glue them onto the mud and the pond.

Pond Animals: Invite students to cut pictures of fish and insects from magazines (or draw pictures) to glue onto the pond. Attach around the pond several turtles from "Painted Turtles" on page 50.

Space

Earth Pictures

Do your little ones know that we live on Earth and that we're surrounded by space? This art activity makes the concept a bit easier to understand. If desired, show students a globe and tell them it's a model of Earth, our planet. Point out your location as well as the oceans and landmasses on the globe. Explain that space surrounds Earth, and when we look into the sky, we're seeing space. Next, give each child a sheet of paper and ask him to draw himself standing outside looking into the night sky. Invite him to color his sky dark blue; then give him a moon sticker and several star stickers to place in the sky. Twinkle, twinkle!

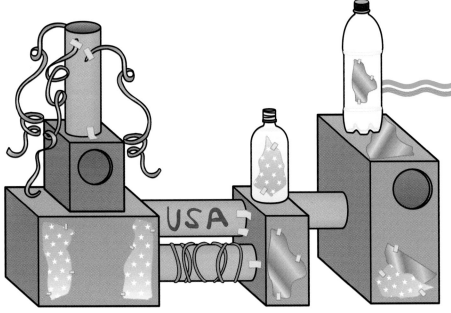

Space Station Sculpture

Here's a sculpture guaranteed to make your youngsters' imaginations soar! Ask parents to send in a variety of clean, interesting items such as cardboard boxes and tubes, plastic bottles and containers, shiny wrapping paper, bubble wrap, ribbons, and so forth. Arrange the items for easy student access along with glue, scissors, and tape. Explain to students that when astronauts go into space for long periods of time they sometimes stay in space stations. Further explain that youngsters will work together to build a class space station. Then invite each small group, in turn, to work on the space station. When the station is finished, take a photo of your little engineers with their creation and then display it where all can enjoy it. Far out!

Starlight Game

Star light, star bright, play this game with a flashlight! Have students stand in a circle. Choose a volunteer to be the star. Have her stand in the middle of the circle holding a flashlight. Lead the rest of the group in saying the rhyme below. At the end of the rhyme, invite the star to shine the light on a child; that child becomes the next star. Continue in this manner until each child has had a turn to be the star.

Star light, star bright,
Shining far and near,
Won't you please shine on me?
Shine your light right here.

Starry Sets

This math game is out of this world! Using the star pattern on page 61, trace a star onto tagboard and cut it out. On each point of the star, draw a different dot set from one to five to make a gameboard. Program five clothespins with numbers from 1 to 5. Next, make a set of cards with the number words from *one* to *five.* Place them facedown with the gameboard and clothespins nearby. To play, a child selects the top card, turns it over, and reads the number word. He finds the matching number clothespin and clips it to the matching dot set. He continues in this manner until each set is matched. Your youngsters' set-matching skills will soon sparkle!

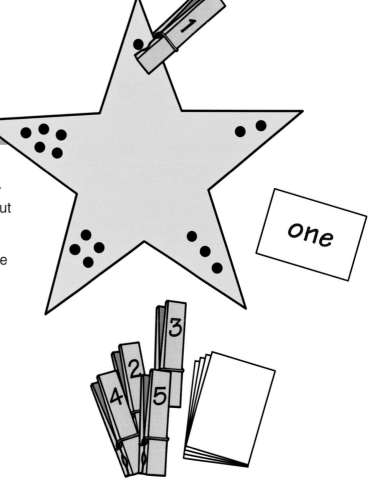

Nine Little Planets

Read the following rhyme aloud to youngsters. If desired, copy the rhyme onto a chart and add a picture of each planet. Then point to the planets as you read.

Nine little planets orbit the sun.
Our first stop is Mercury, planet number one.

Nine little planets are orbiting, it's true.
Our second stop is Venus, planet number two.

Nine little planets, how many can you see?
Our third stop is Earth, planet number three.

Nine little planets, through outer space they soar.
Our fourth stop is Mars, planet number four.

Nine little planets, are we still alive?
Our fifth stop is Jupiter, planet number five.

Nine little planets, our eyes aren't playing tricks.
Our sixth stop is Saturn, planet number six.

Nine little planets, we're flying through the heavens.
Our seventh stop is Uranus, planet number seven.

Nine little planets, we don't want to be late.
Our eighth stop is Neptune, planet number eight.

Nine little planets, each one very fine.
Our ninth stop is Pluto, planet number nine.

shiny

A Galaxy of Words

What words can your little ones use to describe stars? Find out with this twinkly bulletin board display! Copy the star pattern on page 61 onto yellow paper to make a supply. Cut out the stars and store them in your group area. During circle time, ask youngsters to think about stars and the words that can describe them. Guide students to give words and phrases such as *shiny, twinkling, far away, sparkly,* and so forth. As each word or phrase is named, write it on a separate star. Mount the words and phrases on a bulletin board covered in dark blue or black paper. Then read each word or phrase aloud with the class.

Dramatic Play

Inspire some intergalactic building in the block center! Add a poster of the solar system and pictures of space stations, rockets, shuttles, and mission control. Then encourage students in this center to build their own spaceships, space stations, and rockets. You may wish to provide construction paper, scissors, and tape so that youngsters can make unique signs and accessories for their structures. Too cool!

Space Food

The food that astronauts eat in space sometimes looks different from the foods that we enjoy on Earth. Explain to students that some space foods are dehydrated. Then give students an opportunity to explore some dried foods and their fresh counterparts. For example, provide dried apple bits and chopped fresh apples and small portions of beef jerky and roast beef cold cuts. Have children notice how each pair is similar and different. Then invite students to taste each pair and compare the texture and flavor of the fresh and dehydrated foods. For fun, also show children Tang drink mix powder and mix up a pitcher. Serve each child a cup to enjoy with her snack. While children eat, explain that in space, astronauts add water to the dehydrated foods so they taste and look more normal. Anybody want seconds?

Wrapping It Up

Trip to the Moon

Oh boy! Let's take an exciting trip to the moon. Don't forget to pack your imagination!

Oxygen Tanks: Collect a pair of clean, empty two-liter bottles for each child. Remove the labels and tape the bottles together with duct tape. Add ribbon shoulder straps. Invite each child to decorate her oxygen pack with patriotic designs.

Paper Bag Space Helmets: Collect a paper grocery bag for each child. Open the bag and roll down the edges until it is a manageable size. Cut an opening for the face; then have each child use crayons and markers to decorate her helmet.

Space Badges: No space mission is complete without a unique mission badge. Photocopy the badge patterns on page 61 to make a class supply. Cut out the badges and have each child color one. Tape the badge to her shirt or helmet.

Blastoff: Turn a large appliance box into a spaceship. Turn it on its side to make a shuttle or stand it upright to make a rocket. Cut out two doors (on opposite sides) and windows. Enlist student help to decorate the spaceship with paint, markers, and crayons. Invite a small group of astronauts to suit up and join you in the ship. Count backward to blast off and then pretend to fly to the moon.

Lunar Landing: On one side of the spaceship, lay pillows and cushions to create a bumpy, soft moon surface. Cover the surface with an old sheet. Invite students to exit the spaceship on the lunar side and try walking on the moon. After they finish exploring, have them return to the ship for the ride home.

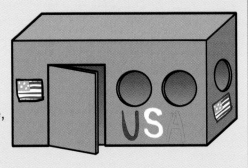

Home Again: When a group of astronauts returns from space, have each crew member draw pictures and write (or dictate as you write) to describe her outer space adventures.

Badge Patterns
Use with "Space Badges" on page 60.

Places in My World Parade

Plan a Places in My World Parade with youngsters. Divide students into four groups; then assign each group a different place from the list below. Use the ideas given for each place to make costumes and props. Then teach youngsters the song on page 63 and let the parade begin!

Farm: Invite youngsters to wear animal ear headbands and make animal sounds. (To make a headband, attach ear-shaped cutouts to a construction paper strip fitted to the child's head.) Have students carry their farm animal puppets or scarecrows from the activities on page 36.

Ocean: Guide two students to hold a length of blue fabric and move it up and down to represent ocean waves. Have the remaining youngsters carry seashells or their paper plate fish from page 44.

Pond: Encourage youngsters to hop along and ribbit like little frogs. Have students carry their water lilies or turtle projects from page 50.

Space: Invite children to wear the space helmets, badges, and oxygen tanks from the activities on page 60. Have some youngsters carry a star from "A Galaxy of Words" on page 58. Encourage students to pretend to float in space as they walk in the parade.

Places in My World Parade Song

(sung to the tune of "When Johnny Comes Marching Home")

The children are marching into town. Hooray! Hooray!
The children are marching in a fun places parade!
First come children from down on the farm
With hens and horses in a big red barn.
Oh, we're so glad the children could come today.

The children are marching into town. Hooray! Hooray!
The children are marching in a fun places parade.
Next come fish from the ocean blue,
Sharks, sea stars, and dolphins too.
Oh, we're so glad the children could come today.

The children are marching into town. Hooray! Hooray!
The children are marching in a fun places parade.
The pond is home to birds and frogs,
And beavers build dams from nearby logs.
Oh, we're so glad the children could come today.

The children are marching into town. Hooray! Hooray!
The children are marching in a fun places parade.
With space gear they'll fly to the moon
To see planets and stars, then return very soon.
Oh, we're so glad the children could come today.

Sun and Shadows

Sun Masks

Let the sun shine in with these adorable masks! To prepare, cut the centers from a class supply of paper plates. Give each youngster a prepared plate and access to yellow construction paper triangles and glue. Have him color the rim orange. Next, help him glue triangles around the rim of his plate to resemble sun rays. Then have him add a craft stick handle and set his mask aside to dry. Later, invite each child to hold his mask in front of his face and dance around the room pretending to be sunshine. How cheerful!

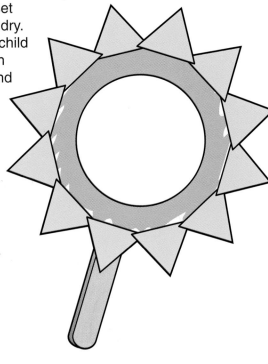

Swirly Suns

Brighten up your classroom with plenty of fingerpainted sunshine! Give each child in a small group a sheet of fingerpaint paper. Then put a spoonful each of yellow and orange finger-paint on each paper. Invite each youngster to swirl the colors together and paint her entire paper. When the paint is dry, help her cut out a large sun shape. Display the suns around your classroom for a little extra sunshine.

Shadow Dancing

This movement opportunity is sure to captivate your little performers! Shine a bright light on a large blank wall. Have a small group of children stand in front of the light and observe their shadows on the wall. Ask them to make their shadows move slowly, then quickly. Have them make their shadows jump up and down. Then ask them to make their shadows stand on one foot. Play some lively music and have the group members make their shadows dance. Repeat with each small group in turn.

Measuring Shadows

Youngsters will explore how shadows measure up throughout the day. Select an object that casts a long shadow outdoors, such as a flagpole or tree. Take your little ones outside on a sunny day and have them observe the shadow. Enlist a volunteer's help to measure the shadow and mark it with a small object, such as a block; then record the measurement on a chart along with the time. Return to the shadow each hour to observe, measure, and record as described above. Discuss the changes throughout the day. Did the shadow get shorter or longer? Did it move away from the starting place? Explain to youngsters that the earth moves around the sun each day, which makes shadows change.

Flagpole Shadow

10:00 Four feet
11:00 Three feet
12:00 Two feet
1:00 Three feet

Good Morning, Ms. Sun

Encourage youngsters to wear their sun masks (see "Sun Masks" on page 64) while you read this poem. Later, teach little ones the poem and recite it together.

Good morning, Ms. Sun.
We're so happy our day's begun.
Your bright rays chase away the gray
So we can have some fun.

Good morning, Ms. Sun.
We hope that you won't run.
We hope you'll stay so we can play
Outside in the warm, bright sun.

Shadow Puppets

Enjoy a little shadow play with plenty of student involvement! To prepare, copy the puppet patterns on page 69 onto construction paper. Cut out each puppet and attach a craft stick handle. Have two children hold the puppets while kneeling in front of a blank wall. Invite another child to shine a bright flashlight on the twosome. Darken your classroom. Then enlist student help in singing the song shown while the puppeteers and light bearer move as directed.

(sung to the tune of "The Itsy-Bitsy Spider")

The little shadow puppets
Danced across the wall,
Sometimes big
And sometimes small.
When the bright light
Started to fall,
The little shadow puppets
Were not there at all.

Dramatic Play

Night meets day in this dramatic-play center! Stock the center with clothing and props for both night and day play. For example, for day play, have sunglasses, a trowel and artificial flowers to use in planting a garden, and clothes to hang on a clothes-line. For night play, have pajamas and robes, a flash-light, and a blanket and pillow. Invite each group of visitors to this center to take turns acting out day and night scenes.

Sunny Snacks

Here are a few ideas for sun snacks:
- sun tea
- lemonade
- sun-shaped sugar cookies with yellow sprinkles or frosting
- cheese slices cut into sun shapes

Sunny Days

Enjoy these sun and shadow explorations with your little ones!

Ice Cube Meltdown: Is it warmer in the sun or in the shade? Invite youngsters to find out with this warm-weather experiment. Place an ice cube in each of two clear plastic cups. Put one cup in the shade and one cup in a sunny location nearby. Have youngsters note that both ice cubes are frozen and hard. Every ten minutes, have students check the cups to see how the cubes are melting. Guide students to notice that the ice cube placed in the sun melts faster than the one in the cooler shade.

Telling Time With the Sun: Make this simple sundial to help illustrate the movement of the sun's light each day. Place a paper plate on the ground in a protected, sunny location. (Make sure the spot receives sun all day.) Then push a thin dowel or pencil through the center of the plate into the ground. Every hour, take children out to the sundial and have a volunteer make a mark on the plate where the dowel's shadow falls. The next day, compare the marked sundial to a clock. Are the marks similar?

Sun Print Pictures: On a sunny, calm day, take youngsters outside to write their names with sunshine! Give each child a sheet of dark-colored construction paper and letter cutouts to spell her name. Help her arrange and tape the cutouts on her paper to spell her name. Leave the paper in the sun for several hours. Then have her remove the cutouts, revealing the child's name. Explain that the sun faded the dark color on the paper. The cutouts blocked the sunlight, leaving her name dark.

Snow

Snowpal Scenes

"Snow" one can resist these seasonal snowpal scenes! Give each youngster a copy of the snowpal pattern on page 75. Have her glue the cutout to a sheet of blue construction paper. Then encourage her to decorate the snowpal with paper embellishments. Have her place the picture in a shallow box and then dip a toothbrush in diluted white paint. Then prompt her to tap the brush with her index finger to spatter paint over the snowpal and the surrounding paper. Remove the picture from the box and set it aside to dry. After the pictures are dry, display them in your classroom. Let it snow!

Frosty Puppets

Brrr! These snowpal puppets look as though they've been outside on a frosty night! Use the pattern on page 75 as a guide to make a construction paper snowpal for each child. Invite each youngster to draw any desired decorations on his snowpal. Then encourage students to brush a mixture of equal parts water and epsom salts onto the snowpal. Allow time for the mixture to dry. Then help each youngster attach a jumbo craft stick to the snowpal to make a puppet. What frosty fun!

Four Little Snowpals

What do four little snowpals do on a chilly day? Your students find out when they recite this fun chant! If desired, make flannelboard props by cutting out four white construction paper snowpals (using the pattern on page 75 as a guide if needed). Draw a face on each snowpal and ready the cutouts for flannelboard use. Then lead youngsters in reciting the chant, removing each cutout when indicated.

Four little snowpals went out to play.
One put on skates and skated away.
Three little snowpals went out to play.
One jumped on a sled and rode away.
Two little snowpals went out to play.
One put on skis and skied away.
One little snowpal went out to play.
He strapped on snowshoes and walked away.

Sorting Clothes

Winter clothing or summer clothing? With this sorting idea, your little ones choose appropriate clothing for each season! Collect a variety of clothing that youngsters associate with winter or summer, such as earmuffs, mittens, coats, shorts, sandals, and sunglasses. Label one container "Winter" and another container "Summer" as shown. Then place the clothing and containers in a center. Invite youngsters to visit the center and sort each item of clothing into the appropriate container. Youngsters are sure to feel they can dress successfully for either season!

Great Big Snowman

This cute little song is just the thing to get your little ones up and moving! Lead students in singing the song below several times. When they are comfortable with the song, encourage them to add the movements.

(sung to the tune of "I'm a Little Teapot")

I'm a great big snowman, round and white.

I stand all day and all through the night.
I am made of snow that's packed and rolled.
I just love it out in the cold!

*Hold arms out to
demonstrate roundness.
Stand very still with arms out.
Pretend to pack a snowball.
Point to self; then shiver.*

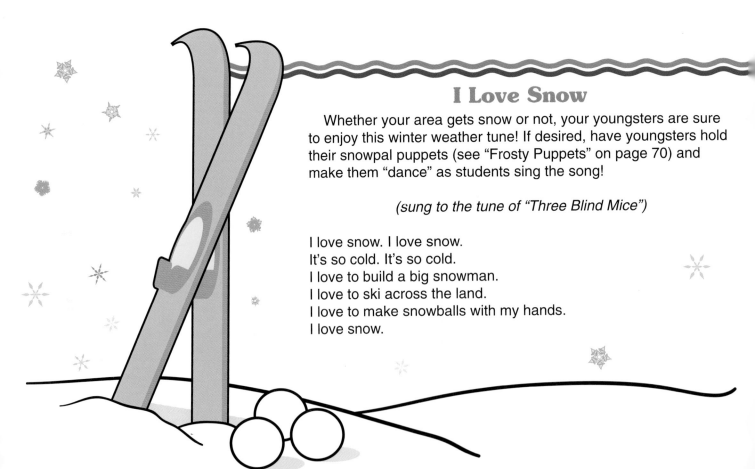

I Love Snow

Whether your area gets snow or not, your youngsters are sure to enjoy this winter weather tune! If desired, have youngsters hold their snowpal puppets (see "Frosty Puppets" on page 70) and make them "dance" as students sing the song!

(sung to the tune of "Three Blind Mice")

I love snow. I love snow.
It's so cold. It's so cold.
I love to build a big snowman.
I love to ski across the land.
I love to make snowballs with my hands.
I love snow.

Dramatic Play

Pretending to play in the snow can be just as much fun as the real thing! Attach a large white sheet to the floor in your dramatic-play area to represent the snowy ground. Then add several props, such as a sled, mittens, boots, winter coats, and a large white box (snow fort). Invite youngsters to the center to dress up in winter garb, play in the snow fort, and go on a pretend sled ride. Whee!

Fluffy Snowpal Snack

You'll receive a flurry of thank-yous when youngsters make these snowpal snacks! Each youngster spreads marshmallow creme on each of three vanilla wafers and arranges them, as shown, to resemble a snowpal. She places mini chocolate chip features on her snowpal. Then she digs into this tasty and simple snack. Yum!

Experimenting With Snow
Snow isn't required for these fun and frosty investigations!

Exploring Measurement: Place a large supply of cotton balls (snow) in a plastic tub. Provide measuring cups and containers in various sizes. Encourage students to count as they use the measuring cups to scoop snow into the containers.

Melting: Fill a bowl with snow (or crushed ice) and place it in your classroom. Invite students to predict how long the snow will take to melt. Have youngsters periodically check the bowl throughout the day. When the snow is completely melted, encourage students to determine whether their predictions were accurate.

Refreeze It: Ask youngsters whether it's possible to turn the water left over from the idea above back into snow. Have youngsters suggest ways they might accomplish this. Then help them follow through with some of the suggestions, such as placing the container of water outside or in the freezer. Encourage students to discuss why the water turned into ice rather than snow.

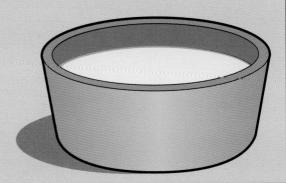

Wind

Kite Puppets

Little ones will soar with the wind when they make these cute kite puppets! Make a tagboard copy of the kite and bow patterns on page 81 for each student. Invite each youngster to color the bows and decorate her kite with a face. Help her tape a craft stick and an eight-inch length of crepe paper to the bottom of the kite. Then have her glue the bows onto the crepe paper. When the glue is dry, take your little kite flyers outside to watch their kites' tails blow in the wind!

Windy Pictures

This blustery art project is sure to delight youngsters' artistic sides! Fill each of two squeeze bottles with a different color of diluted tempera paint. Give each child a 12" x 18" sheet of construction paper and help him squirt a small amount of each paint color onto his paper. Instruct each youngster to gently blow into a straw, directing the air to spread the paint on his paper. After the paint dries, display these unique windy projects for all to see!

[One] little kite(s), flying in the sun,
Waved to a friend to join in the fun.

Flying Kites

Youngsters will be flying high during this circle-time game! Seat little ones in a large circle and choose one child to act as a kite. Have the kite stand in the middle of the circle and pretend to fly around. Lead youngsters in the provided rhyme. Then, at the end of the verse, have the kite wave to another student and invite her to join him inside the circle. Continue reciting additional verses, substituting the appropriate number word in the first line, until five students are inside the circle. Have the group sit down; then choose another kite and repeat the rhyme until all youngsters have had an opportunity to "fly."

Heavy Versus Light

Acting as the wind is a great way for students to experiment with heavy and light objects. At a center, place two empty containers, one labeled "heavy," with a picture of a rock, and the other labeled "light," with a picture of a feather. Also, place at the center a container with a variety of small objects that are heavy and light, such as a tissue, a piece of paper, a feather, a cotton ball, a leaf, a rock, a block, an eraser, and a toy car. Instruct each center visitor to choose an object, place it on a table, and then blow on it. Have him observe the object to see whether it moved easily (a light object) or whether it did not move (a heavy object). Then instruct him to place the object in the corresponding container. No doubt, youngsters are sure to drift by this center again and again!

Huffing and Puffing

Use the classic story *The Three Little Pigs* to get youngsters in the mood to do some huffing, puffing, and blowing of their own! After reading aloud any version of the story, discuss the idea that heavy winds can blow down some things that are light, but it is more difficult to blow down things that are heavy. Show students how to use cotton swabs, craft sticks, and DUPLO blocks to build two-dimensional houses as shown. Have students guess which house will be the easiest to blow apart and which house will be the most difficult. Invite a volunteer to blow on each house while students observe the results. Reconstruct the houses that were blown apart and encourage other volunteers to blow with different strengths. If desired, place the materials at a center and invite students to build houses and blow them apart.

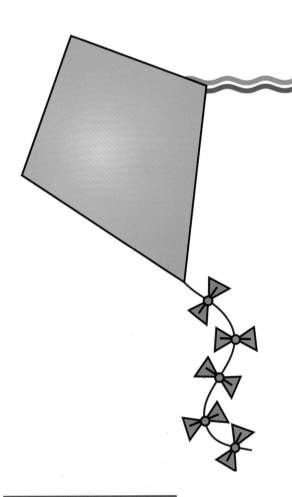

Kites Are Flying

Kite flying is more fun when youngsters sing this little ditty!

(sung to the tune of "Frére Jacques")

Kites are flying; kites are flying
In the sky, in the sky.
They dip and soar around
And glide above the ground,
Way up high, in the sky.

Dramatic Play

Your little wind watchers will be blown away by this dramatic-play activity! All you need is a windy day and a two-foot length of ribbon for each student. On a windy day, take students outside and have them observe what happens to lengths of ribbon when they are let go. After they see the ribbon drift to the ground, invite students to hold onto their ribbons and move them around in the wind. Encourage youngsters to act as the wind helping their ribbons soar. What a fun way to make the best of a windy day!

Windy Whipped Cream Snack

Whip up a creamy treat for young-sters using "wind" (air moved around by a mixer)! Show students two cups of whipping cream. Explain that when air is added to the cream, it will become whipped cream. Pour the cream into a mixing bowl and whip it with an electric mixer until the liquid becomes fluffy whipped cream. Add sugar to sweeten, as desired. Encourage students to observe the change that occurred and discuss what they saw. Give each youngster a spoonful of whipped cream along with fresh fruit slices to enjoy as an airy treat.

Wrapping It Up

Simple Windy Experiments

Experimenting with wind is a breeze with these windy activities!

Spinning Spiral: Give each student a six-inch paper plate to decorate as desired. Cut each student's decorated paper plate into a spiral, as shown, and punch a hole in the center of the plate. Tie a length of string through the hole. Pair students and have one child hold the spiral by the string. Instruct the other student to act as the wind and blow on the spiral. Encourage youngsters to observe the way the spiral moves. Have partners switch roles and repeat the activity. If desired, take students outside on a windy day to observe their spirals in the wind.

Windy Boat Float: Get your water table ready for a boat float! Give each student a six-inch square of aluminum foil. Help each youngster fold his foil into a boat shape. Invite two students at a time to place their boats in the water table. Direct youngsters to move their boats across the water by blowing on them. Encourage little ones to try different ways of blowing to determine the quickest way to move their boats.

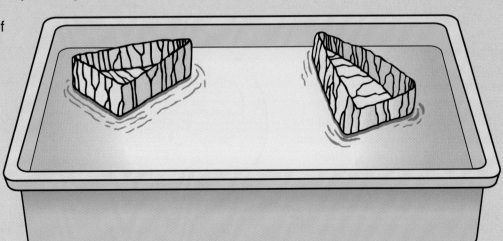

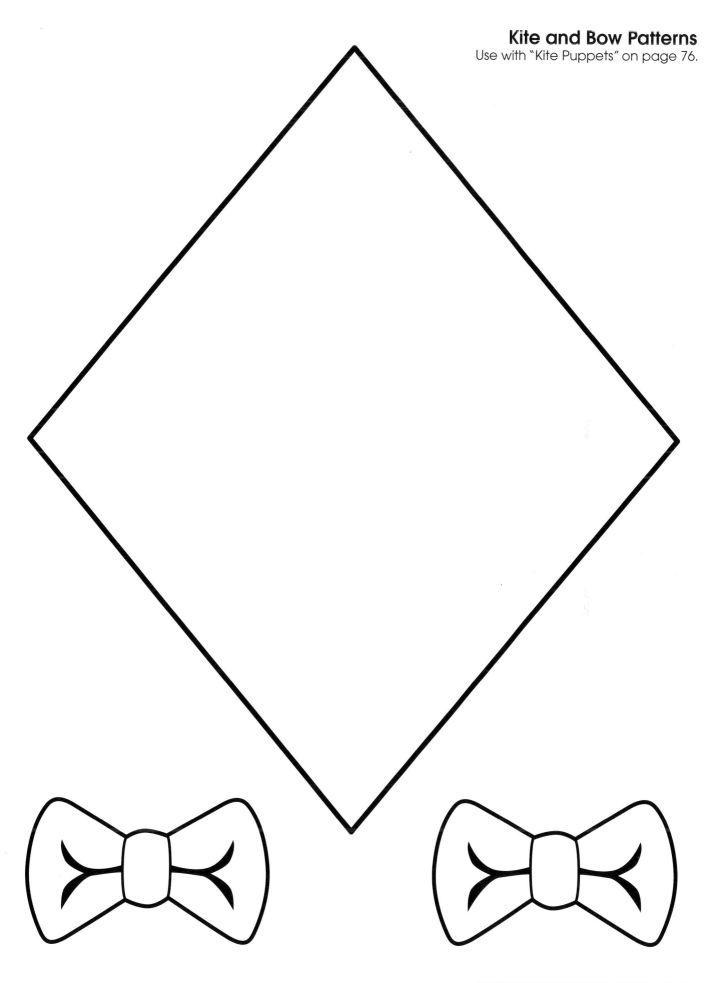

Clouds

Cloudy Day Pictures

Clouds can be all over the sky, even blocking the sun. These cloudy day pictures will allow youngsters to choose where to place clouds in the sky. Invite each student to draw a sunny outdoor scene on a sheet of light blue construction paper. Direct each youngster to stretch out two cotton balls and glue them on the sky in any one of the following locations: over the sun, partially over the sun, or not over the sun at all. Encourage little ones to share their pictures and describe where the clouds are located. If desired, enlist students' help in sorting the pictures by cloud location; then display each group together on a bulletin board.

Painting Rain Clouds

Youngsters are sure to have their hands in the clouds with this art activity! Explain that sometimes gray clouds in the sky mean that rain is on the way. Then give each student a sheet of white construction paper with a spoonful of black paint and a spoonful of white paint. Have her mix the colors together with her fingers (making gray paint) as she covers the entire paper with paint. When the paint is dry, have each child cut out a large cloud shape from her painted paper. Next, direct her to glue strips of blue crepe paper to the bottom of the cloud to represent rain. Display the rain clouds on a window to make any day a rainy one!

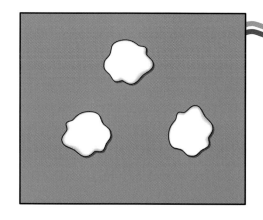

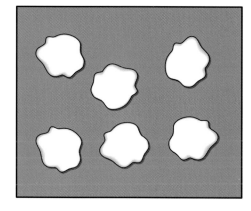

Counting Clouds

Fluffy clouds are for counting at this math center! On each of six pieces of blue construction paper, glue a different number of cotton balls from one to six to make cloud cards. Program six smaller cards each with a different numeral from 1 to 6. Store each set of cards in a different container. Place both containers at a center. When a child visits the center, he removes the number cards and spreads them out on the table. Then he removes one cloud card, counts the cotton balls, and finds the matching number card. He continues in this manner for the remaining cards. What a great way to make counting practice a breeze!

Directional Clouds

Where are the clouds? On the flannelboard, of course! Cut four cloud shapes from white felt and use the pattern on page 87 to make one felt airplane. Place the airplane in the middle of the flannelboard and the clouds beside the flannelboard. Give a direction such as "Place two clouds below the airplane" or "Place one cloud above the airplane." Invite a volunteer to follow the direction by positioning the cloud(s) in the corresponding location on the flannelboard. Remove the clouds and continue in this manner until each student has had a turn. If desired, place the felt cutouts at a center for students to practice using directional words with a partner.

What Could It Be?

A cloudy day is a perfect day to have your little ones drift outside and observe the many different shapes of clouds! As youngsters observe the clouds, encourage them to discuss with a partner objects that the clouds look like. After returning to the classroom, instruct each student to draw one thing she saw in the clouds on white construction paper; then help her cut it out and glue it on blue paper. Gather students in a circle and invite each youngster to hold up her project; then have the other students guess what it is. After each student shows her cloud, write her name and what her cloud is on the back of the project. Encourage each youngster to take her cloud home and have family members guess what the cloud is!

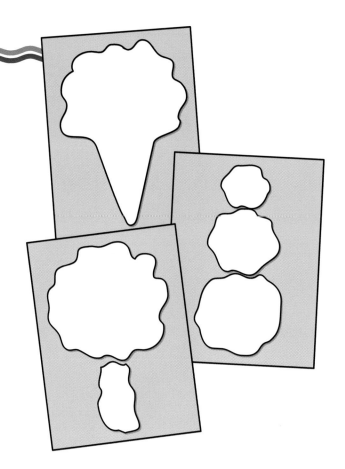

I'm a Little Cloud

Introduce your little cloudgazers to how clouds are different with this catchy song!

(sung to the tune of "I'm a Little Teapot")

I'm a little cloud up in the sky.
Sometimes I'm low, and sometimes I'm high.
I can be wispy, puffy, or gray.
I just love to float all day!

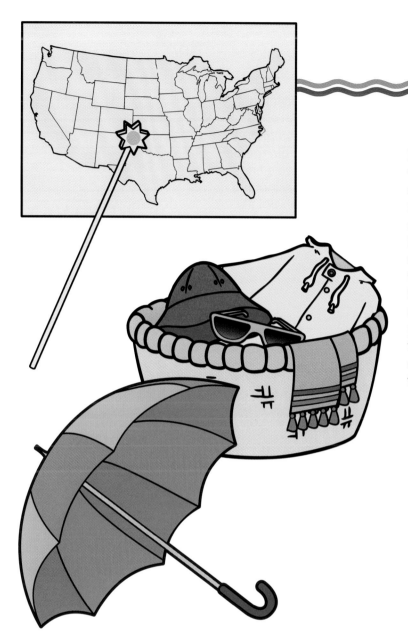

Dramatic Play

Delight your young weather forecasters by turning your dramatic-play area into a weather center! After discussing the role of a weather forecaster, set out weather-related items such as laminated maps, a child-safe pointer, and seasonal clothing. Invite a pair of students to the center and encourage one student to create a weather forecast and the other student to dress up for the weather forecast. Then have them switch roles. If desired, have the twosome present one of the weather forecasts to the class. Youngsters don't need to worry about the weather to have a good time at this center!

Creamy, Dreamy Cloud Snacks

This simple snacktime activity will provide your little ones with a delicious cloudlike treat! Provide each student with a sheet of waxed paper labeled with his name. Place a large scoop of nondairy whipped topping on each sheet. Encourage each youngster to use a plastic spoon to create a unique cloud shape; then have him embellish his cloud with blue sprinkles to represent rain. Freeze the clouds overnight; then remove them from the freezer and enjoy!

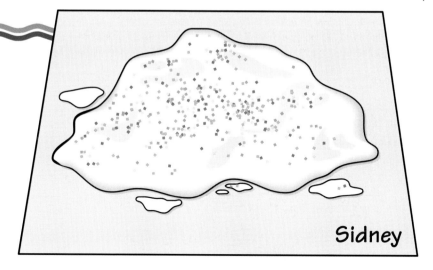

Sidney

Wrapping It Up

Cloudy Day Fun

Little ones act as different clouds when they perform this movement activity! Prior to the activity, send home a note asking that each child dress in all white on a specified day. Enlarge the cloud cards on page 87 and glue each to a separate sheet of blue construction paper. On the day of the activity, display the cards on the board. Recite the following lines, pointing to the corresponding card, and guide youngsters in performing the movements. If desired, invite families to come and watch their little clouds perform this movement activity.

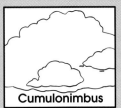

Cumulonimbus Clouds
Thunder clouds, thunder clouds, reach up high,
Dark and scary up in the sky.

Reach hands up.
Move arms and hands slowly in the air.

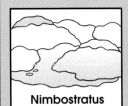

Nimbostratus Clouds
Rain clouds, rain clouds, way down low,

Dampening everything down below.

Bend over, stretch out arms, and point fingers down.
Wiggle fingers on the ground.

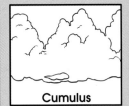

Cumulus Clouds
Puffy clouds, puffy clouds, fluffy and round,
Gliding along without a sound.

Puff up cheeks.
Stretch arms out and sway from side to side.

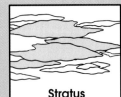

Stratus Clouds
Flat clouds, flat clouds, long and thin,

Not letting all the sunlight in.

Stand up straight and stretch out arms.
Hook hands together with others.

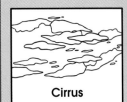

Cirrus Clouds
Wispy clouds, wispy clouds, high in the sky,
Rain or snow may soon be by.

Wiggle fingers in the air.
Move hands slowly down while wiggling fingers.

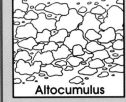

Altocumulus Clouds
Popcorn clouds, popcorn clouds, round and small,
Clustered together like little balls.

Squat down into a ball.
Move together to make a cluster.

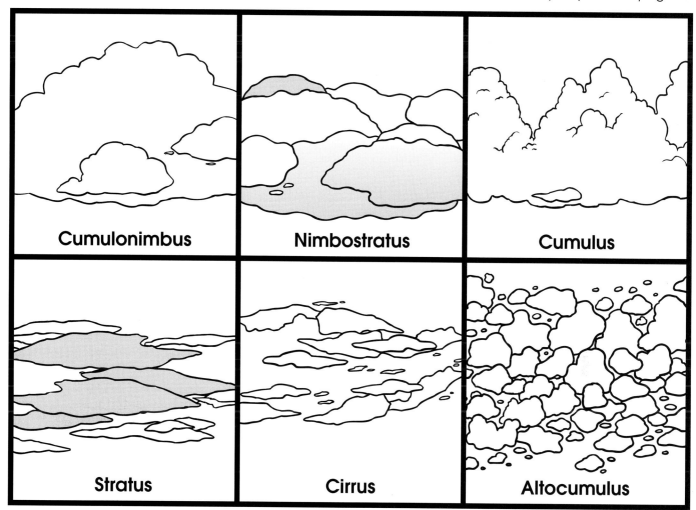

Cumulonimbus

Nimbostratus

Cumulus

Stratus

Cirrus

Altocumulus

Airplane Pattern
Use with "Directional Clouds" on page 83.

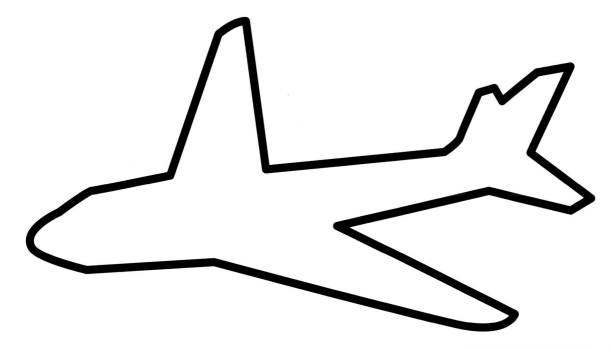

Rain and Rainbows

Colorful Rainbows

Brighten the classroom as youngsters practice color matching with this cheery art project. Program a sheet of paper with an uncolored rainbow and then make a white construction paper copy for each child, plus one for yourself. Color your copy of the rainbow to create a color guide as shown. Next, cut out a supply of small squares of red, orange, yellow, green, blue, and purple tissue paper. Set out crayons, a shallow dish of water-diluted glue, and paintbrushes. Ask each child to color his rainbow to match the sample. Next, have each child brush glue over his colored rainbow. Then have him match colored tissue paper squares to each section of his rainbow as shown. When the glue is dry, display the rainbows around a window in the classroom.

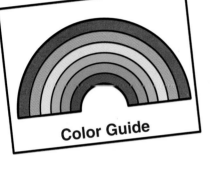

Color Guide

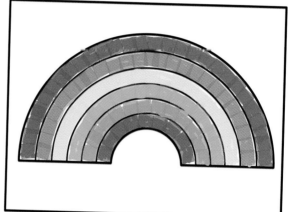

Rain Cloud Windsocks

Shower the classroom with these rain cloud creations! Set out a supply of cotton balls and glue. Give each child a 3" x 18" gray construction paper strip and six-inch light blue crepe paper strips. Have each child stretch several cotton balls and glue them onto the gray strip to form clouds. Next, help each student lay her strip cloud side down and glue the crepe paper strips evenly along the horizontal edge. When the glue is dry, connect the ends of the gray strip to form a cylinder and secure it with tape. Punch two holes at the top of the cloud and attach a yarn hanger as shown.

Five Little Raindrops

Counting backward is lots of fun with this rainy rhyme! Cut five raindrop shapes from light blue felt and place them on a flannelboard. Help youngsters count the raindrops as you point to each one. Then ask a child to remove one raindrop at a time as you read aloud the corresponding verse in the rhyme.

Five little raindrops, up in a cloud,
Are ready to jump; their mothers are so proud.

The first one jumped and said, "Watch me!"
As she fell down to the sea.

The second one said, "I can do that!"
As he closed his eyes and landed on a hat.

The third one said, "I'm ready too!"
So she held her nose and jumped through the blue.

The fourth one said, "I'm set to go!"
As he jumped, then fell far below.

The fifth one said, "I'm all alone!"
As she jumped down on her own.

Five little raindrops now can rest.
Each has passed the jumping test.

Rainbow Color Game

Youngsters take a spin at color-identification skills with this small-group game. Draw a large rainbow on poster board and color it as shown; then laminate the resulting gameboard for durability. To make a game spinner, color six sections on a paper plate and use a paper fastener to attach a large paper clip as shown. To play, each child in a small group places a game marker below the rainbow. In turn, each child spins the spinner and names the corresponding color. If the color is purple, he moves his marker to the purple arc of the rainbow. If the color is not purple, he does not move his marker. Each child repeats the process, moving his marker in color order on the rainbow. The group continues play until each child has reached the red section of the rainbow.

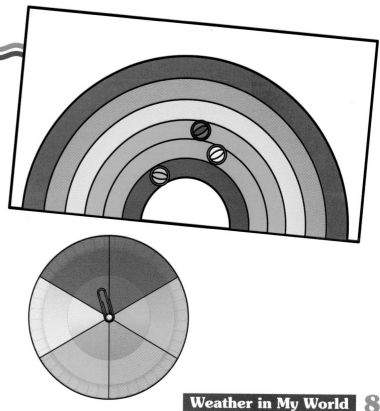

Plip, Plop, Raindrop

Reinforce rhyming skills right down to the last drop of this activity. Make a tagboard copy of the cards on page 93. Color and cut out the cards; then laminate them for durability and prepare them for flannelboard use. Also cut a raindrop shape from blue felt and place it on your flannelboard. Gather your group around the flannelboard and ask them to say the word *raindrop* as you point to the felt drop. Guide them to hear the ending sound *op.* Next, place one card on the flannelboard and have students name the picture. If the word rhymes with *drop,* place it under the raindrop on the flannelboard. If it doesn't rhyme, place it on the opposite side. Repeat the activity with each remaining picture card. As a variation, use this idea to identify the pictures that rhyme with *drip.* Drip, drip, drop!

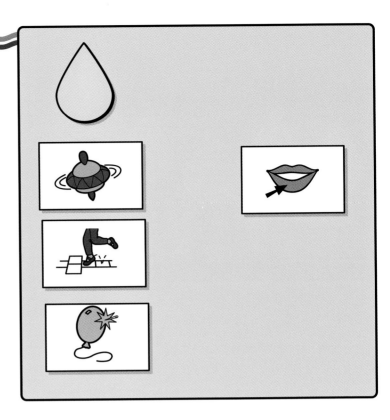

Rain Song

Create a storm of excitement as youngsters act out this rainy day song.

(sung to the tune of "It's Raining; It's Pouring")

It's raining; it's pouring.
Staying inside is boring.
I'll put on my boots and run outside.
Then I'll jump in a puddle, deep and wide!

Dramatic Play

Gearing up for rainy weather promotes creative play and motor skills. Place a box of rain gear, such as raincoats, rain ponchos, rubber boots, rain hats, and umbrellas in your dramatic-play area. Also, cut out several blue construction paper puddles and tape them to the floor in an open area. Set the rainy atmosphere by playing recorded rain sounds. Next, invite several students to help each other button, zip, and snap as they put on the rain gear. Then have each child jump into, jump out of, and jump beside a puddle. Splish, splash!

Rain Cloud Snack

Come rain or shine, this fluffy cloud snack hits the spot! In advance, prepare a package of blue gelatin and purchase a container of whipped topping. Help each child place a scoop of whipped topping in a clear plastic cup to represent a cloud. Next, have her add several cubes of blue gelatin to represent raindrops within the cloud. Then invite each child to enjoy her tasty rain cloud.

Wrapping It Up

Watery Wonders

Use these simple experiments to shower students with exploration experiences.

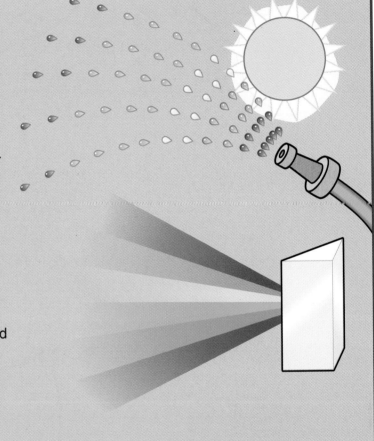

Making Rainbows: Shed light on how raindrops and rainbows are connected with these quick demonstrations. Then explain to students that a rainbow can be seen in the sky when the sun shines on raindrops.

- Tape white paper onto the ceiling. Partially fill a clear jar with water. Shine a flashlight through the bottom of the jar onto the white paper. Slightly angle the light and make gentle waves in the jar to produce a spectrum of color onto the white paper.
- Twirl a prism in the sunlight to reflect rainbow colors on the wall and floor.
- On a sunny day, spray water from a garden hose outdoors. Have each child stand with her back to the sun and help her discover the rainbow colors reflected within the water spray.
- Set a clear glass of water in a sunny window. As the sun shines through the water, hold a sheet of white paper near the glass to capture the reflection of rainbow colors.

Measuring Rain: Make a rain gauge by using a permanent marker to draw one-inch increments on the outside of a plastic jar. Place the rain gauge outside in an open area. At the end of a rainy day, have students check the gauge and help them measure the rainfall. Record the information; then empty the rain gauge and repeat the activity on another day.

Weather in My World Parade

Plan a Weather All Around Me Parade with youngsters. Divide students into five groups; then assign each group a different type of weather from the list below. Use the ideas given for each weather type to make costumes and props. Then teach youngsters the song on page 95 and let the parade begin!

Sun and Shadows: Invite students to wear sunglasses and sun hats and carry beach bags. Have several youngsters wear their masks from "Sun Masks" on page 64. Have other students carry their puppets from "Shadow Puppets" on page 66.

Snow: Encourage youngsters to wear mittens and stocking caps. Have students carry their puppets from "Frosty Puppets" on page 70 and toss cotton ball snowballs.

Wind: Assign a leader of this group and have her wear a windbreaker and wave a flag. Have other students fly their puppets from "Kite Puppets" on page 76.

Clouds: Have students carry fluffy white pillows to represent clouds.

Rain and Rainbows: Invite several youngsters to wear rain boots and raincoats and carry umbrellas. Have other students carry their rainbows or windsocks from the activities on page 88.

Weather in My World Parade Song

(sung to the tune of "When Johnny Comes Marching Home")

The children are marching into town. Hooray! Hooray!
The children are marching in a great big weather parade.
Some wear boots and carry umbrellas high.
Some carry windsocks and kites that fly.
Oh, we're so glad the children could come today.

The children are marching into town. Hooray! Hooray!
Some toss snowballs as they come our way.
Others carry clouds and colorful rainbows.
Some hold sun masks and wear beach clothes.
Oh, we're so glad the children could come today.

Nursery Rhymes

Mary's Lamb

Mary had a little lamb, and now your little ones can have a little lamb of their own too! Give each student a tagboard cutout of a lamb pattern from page 101. Have each youngster attach two black clothespin legs to the bottom of the lamb. Then direct him to decorate the face with markers and glue on cotton balls to cover the lamb's body. After the glue is dry, encourage little ones to use their lambs as props while reciting the rhyme "Mary Had a Little Lamb." These standing lambs are sure to go many places with youngsters!

Miss Muffet's Spiders

These friendly spiders won't frighten your youngsters away! Have each student turn a small paper soup bowl upside down and paint the outside with black tempera paint. When the paint is dry, give each youngster eight five-inch lengths of black yarn. Help her glue the yarn on the inside rim of the bowl so that the yarn hangs down like spider legs. After the glue dries, have each child glue construction paper eyes and a yarn mouth on the front of the bowl. Poke a hole in the top of the spider and thread a ten-inch length of yarn through the hole. Then knot the yarn inside of the bowl. Encourage little Miss Muffets and Mr. Muffets to retell the related rhyme using their spiders as props.

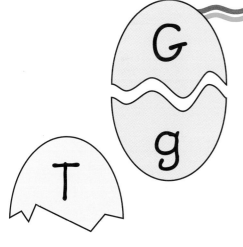

Humpty Dumpty Letter Puzzles

Humpty Dumpty is the inspiration for this letter-matching center! Cut a supply of five-inch egg shapes from different colors of tagboard. Program an uppercase letter on the top of each egg and its corresponding lowercase letter on the bottom; then laminate if desired. Use a different puzzle cut on each egg to separate the letter pairs. Store the egg halves in a container and place it in a center. When a child visits the center, he spreads the egg halves on a table. Then he matches the uppercase and lowercase letters to piece together the egg puzzles. Who said you couldn't put Humpty Dumpty back together again?

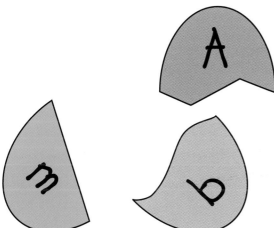

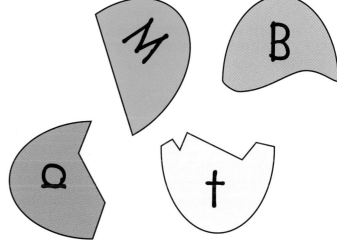

Nursery Rhyme Pairs

Who's Jack without Jill? Or Miss Muffet without the spider? Use this spin on Concentration to have youngsters match nursery rhyme pairs. Make one tagboard copy of the cards on pages 102 and 103 for each pair of students. Review the nursery rhymes displayed on the cards. Then invite little ones to color the pictures and cut out the cards. Next, direct each twosome to mix up the cards and place them facedown in rows. In turn, each student flips over two cards. If the cards make a nursery rhyme match, he keeps them. If they do not match, he turns them back over. Students continue playing in this manner until all the cards are matched. What a fun way to review favorite nursery rhymes!

Nursery Rhyme Riddles

It's nursery rhyme riddle time! Read aloud the following riddles and invite youngsters to use their nursery rhyme knowledge to solve them.

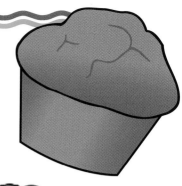

I am sold by the muffin man.
You bake me in a pan.
What am I? *(a muffin)*

The Queen of Hearts baked me on a summer day.
But the Knave of Hearts took me away!
What am I? *(a tart)*

The three little kittens couldn't have me
Because their mittens no one could see.
What am I? *(pie)*

My name is Humpty Dumpty. I fell off a wall.
I break easily when I fall.
What am I? *(an egg)*

Jack and Jill carried me up the hill.
But when they fell, my water did spill.
What am I? *(a pail)*

I had a job to watch the sheep,
But I decided to go to sleep.
Who am I? *(Little Boy Blue)*

A Nursery Rhyme Tune

Sing this rhyming tune to celebrate little ones' enthusiasm for some of their favorite timeless tales.

(sung to the tune of "Jingle Bells")

Nursery rhymes,
Nursery rhymes—
They are so much fun.
I just love to hear them read—
Each and every one!
Little Miss Muffet,
Jack and Jill,
Or the Muffin Man—
I'd like for them
To come and play
Because I'm their biggest fan!

Shopping List

"The Muffin Man": empty muffin tins, muffin liners, empty flour and sugar bags, play dough

"The Queen of Hearts": heart-shaped cookie cutters, cookie sheets, spatulas, empty flour and sugar bags, pink play dough

"Pat-a-Cake": play dough, cake pan, nonserrated plastic knives, empty frosting containers

Dramatic Play

Your little bakers are sure to cook up some nursery rhyme fun when you turn your dramatic-play area into a bakery! Choose a bakery-themed rhyme from the list and place aprons, mixing bowls, spoons, and the additional suggested items in your dramatic-play area to represent the rhyme. Then invite student pairs to use the materials as they act as nursery rhyme bakers. Keep interest high by choosing different nursery rhymes and changing the props.

Nursery Rhyme Snacks

Choose a delicious nursery rhyme treat to serve your little ones at snacktime.

The Queen of Hearts' Fruity Tarts
individual shortcakes (one per student)
canned peaches
strawberry slices
blueberries
whipped topping

Place one peach slice in the shortcake. Add a spoonful of strawberries and a spoonful of blueberries. Top with a spoonful of whipped topping and a strawberry slice.

Little Boy Blue's Haystack
2 packages of butterscotch chips
large package of chow mein noodles

Melt the butterscotch chips on a hot plate or in a microwave. Do not stir. Mix in the chow mein noodles and stir until well-coated. Drop spoonfuls of the mixture onto separate pieces of waxed paper to make one for each student. Refrigerate to cool before serving.

Humpty Dumpty Salad
chilled hard-boiled eggs (one per student)
mayonnaise
salt and pepper (optional)

Crack the egg shell and peel it off. Place the egg in a bowl and mash it with a plastic fork. Stir in a spoonful of mayonnaise. Add a dash of salt and pepper if desired. Serve with crackers.

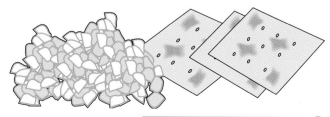

Nursery Rhyme Dramatics

Set aside a special time to celebrate youngsters' love for nursery rhymes with this whole-class activity. In advance, gather the listed props and store them in a large basket or box. Seat little ones in a circle and review the listed nursery rhymes. Then choose a nursery rhyme from the list and invite two volunteers to find the corresponding props. Encourage seated students to recite the nursery rhyme while the volunteers walk around the circle interacting with the props. Continue in this manner, making sure each student gets a turn.

Nursery Rhyme	Props
"Old King Cole"	2 crowns
"Twinkle, Twinkle, Little Star"	2 yellow star cutouts
"Three Little Kittens"	2 pairs of mittens
"The Muffin Man"	muffin tin and an apron
"Mary, Mary, Quite Contrary"	watering can and gardening gloves
"Mary Had a Little Lamb"	2 toy lambs
"Little Miss Muffet"	bowl with a spoon and a toy spider
"Jack Be Nimble"	2 candlesticks
"Jack and Jill"	2 water pails
"Humpty Dumpty"	2 plastic eggs
"Hickory, Dickory, Dock"	toy clock and toy mouse

Nursery Rhyme Cards

Use with "Nursery Rhyme Pairs" on page 97.

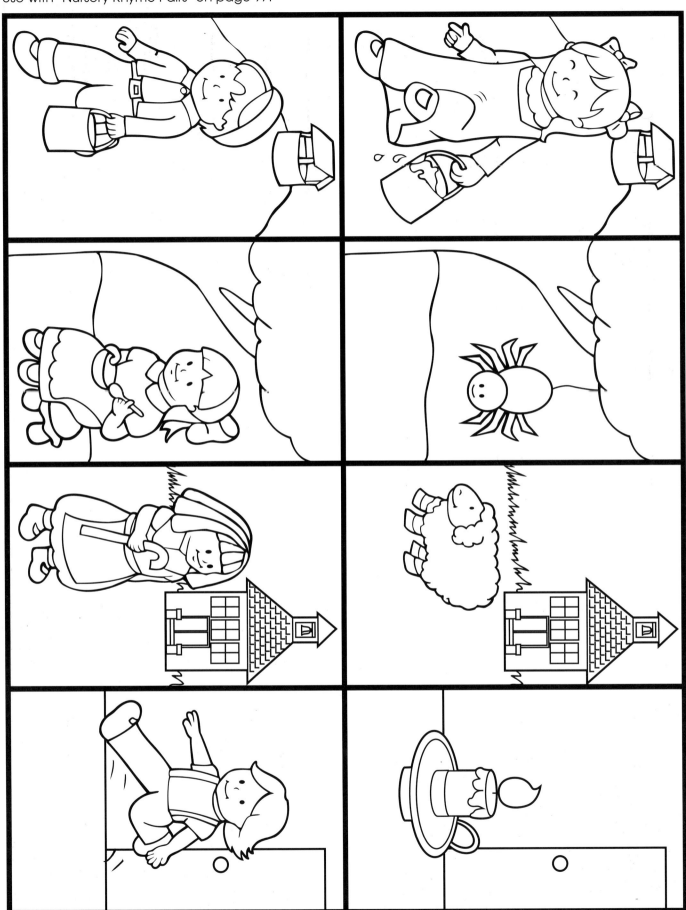

Friends

Friendship Bracelets

Youngsters are eager to accessorize their friends with these simple friendship bracelets! To prepare, cut out a large supply of 1" x 7" construction paper strips in a variety of colors. Place the strips and a supply of stickers at a center. Invite each child to decorate several strips with stickers, one strip for himself and one for each of his friends. Then help him use a sticker to attach each bracelet to a different friend's wrist as shown.

Friendship Play Dough

Mix in a little play dough magic with this clever idea focused on friendship. In advance, make three batches of play dough using the recipe below. Tint a batch in each of the following colors: red, yellow, blue. Divide students into three groups. Give each child in a group a ball of the same color of play dough. Next, invite students to share small pieces of their play dough with friends. Then encourage the groups to mix the colors of dough to make new colors. Neat!

Play Dough

2 c. flour
1 c. salt
1 tbsp. vegetable oil
1 tbsp. food coloring
1 c. water

Mix the first three ingredients in a bowl. Stir together the food coloring and water. Slowly add the tinted water to the flour mixture until a ball forms. Knead the dough until it is soft and pliable.

Puzzle Play

Little friends get together when playing this puzzle game. Break apart enough two-piece puzzles so that each child will have one puzzle piece. Place the pieces in a bag. Have each child, in turn, draw a puzzle piece from the bag. On your cue, have youngsters search for the friend who has the piece to complete the puzzle. When two students find each other, instruct them to put their puzzle together and then say, "We're puzzle pals!" Continue play for more rounds as desired.

Ball Toss

Friendship creates teamwork during this group game. Divide students into groups of four. Give each group a large scarf or square of fabric. Have each child in the group hold one corner of the scarf. Place a foam ball in the center of the scarf and have youngsters work together to toss and catch the ball with the scarf. That's terrific teamwork, friends!

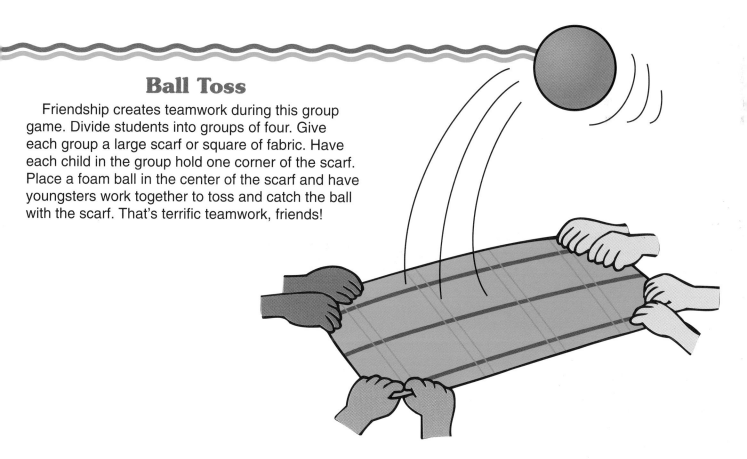

Describe a Friend

This warm and fuzzy idea is sure to have youngsters smiling as they describe friends using complete sentences. During circle time, begin by saying three nice things about a student, such as "Kent draws really well," "He runs really fast," and "He has a great smile." Then encourage him to turn to the person to his right and say three nice things about that child. Encourage compliments around the circle until everyone has had a turn. What a friendly group!

Friends Song

(sung to the tune of "The More We Get Together")

Friends all play together,
Together, together.
Friends all play together, so happily.
There's no hitting or biting,
Or teasing or fighting.
Friends all play together, so happily.

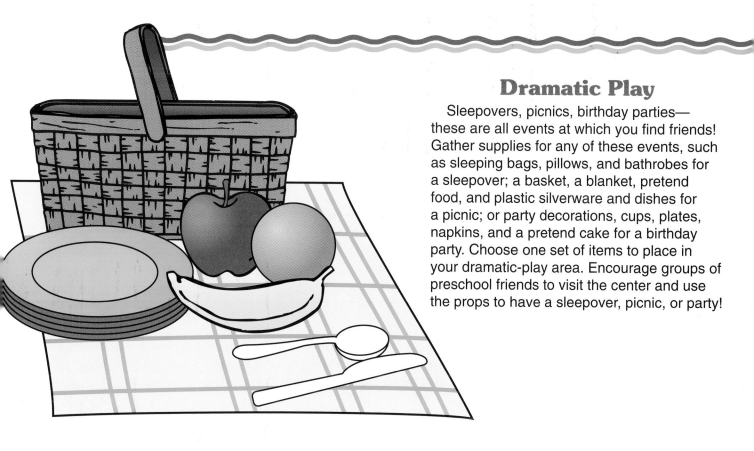

Dramatic Play

Sleepovers, picnics, birthday parties—these are all events at which you find friends! Gather supplies for any of these events, such as sleeping bags, pillows, and bathrobes for a sleepover; a basket, a blanket, pretend food, and plastic silverware and dishes for a picnic; or party decorations, cups, plates, napkins, and a pretend cake for a birthday party. Choose one set of items to place in your dramatic-play area. Encourage groups of preschool friends to visit the center and use the props to have a sleepover, picnic, or party!

Friendly Snack

Snacks taste better when made and shared with a friend! Pair students and have them wash their hands. Give each child a paper plate, a plastic knife, and a slice of bread. Instruct one child to spread butter on her bread slice, and have the other child spread jam on her slice. Help youngsters put the slices of bread together and then cut the resulting sandwich in two. Invite each friend to snack on a half. Yummy!

Wrapping It Up

Friendship Party

Little friends will love to plan a party to celebrate friendships! Use these ideas to help youngsters plan and prepare for a festive friendship party.

Party Decorations: Provide students with streamers, construction paper, stickers, crayons, and glue. Invite them to design and create decorations together to decorate the room. Attach the decorations to walls, tables, and the door.

Party Hats: Purchase basic cone-shaped party hats. Provide youngsters with a variety of collage materials, such as feathers, small silk flowers (without the stems), bows, lengths of ribbon, and paper scraps. Give each child a hat, and have him use craft glue to adhere the materials to it as desired. Allow the glue to dry.

Party Game: Place several adult-size button-up shirts 15 feet from students. Pair youngsters; then divide the pairs into two teams. Show children how each child needs to put one arm in the shirt and then put her other arm around her friend before returning to their team. Play continues until each pair has had a turn to wear a shirt. Encourage lots of cheering as friends participate.

Party Food: Instruct each child to bring one half cup of cereal in a bag to school. (Request cereals without peanut butter to avoid allergy concerns.) Invite each child to pour her cereal pieces into a large bowl. Mix the cereal and then serve this friendship snack in small paper cups. Have children work together to make lemonade to drink.

Party Placemats: Make a white construction paper copy of the placemat on page 109 for each child. Provide youngsters with several stamp pads in a variety of colors. Show students how to use the stamp pads to make thumbprints on their placemats. Have students invite friends to add thumbprints to their mats as well. Then laminate the placemats for durability.

I am "thumb-body's" friend!

Name _Kalen_

I am "thumb-body's" friend!

Name _____

Birthdays

Birthday Party Balloons

Happy birthday to you! In advance, copy the balloon pattern on page 115 onto colorful construction paper to make a class supply. Cut out the balloons and store them near your circle area. Gather little ones and discuss birthday parties and decorations. Lead students to conclude that balloons are popular decorations. Then give each child a balloon cutout and invite him to use glitter glue, markers, crayons, and stamps with washable stamp pads to decorate his birthday balloon. If desired, personalize each balloon with the child's name and his birthday. Tape a length of curling ribbon to the stem of each balloon and mount it on a bulletin board for a cheerful display.

Party Hats

These fashionable party hats are easy to decorate and fun to wear! For each child, cut out a tagboard triangle and a construction paper headband. Set out glue and an assortment of craft materials such as pom-poms, tiny sequins, feathers, foam shapes, and paper die-cuts. Encourage each child to decorate her triangle to resemble a birthday hat. When she is pleased with her hat, help her glue it to her headband. When the glue is dry, complete the headband by taping the ends to fit the student's head.

Birthday Candle Counting

How many candles will each child need on her next birthday cake? Youngsters will find out with this counting activity! To prepare, duplicate the cake and candle patterns on page 116. Color and cut apart the patterns; then laminate them if desired. Have each child in a small group take a turn making a birthday cake for herself. Help her count out candles to match her age; then assist her in adding one candle for her next birthday and counting the total. Wow—you'll be five years old on your next birthday!

A Bunch of Balloons

Here's a bright and cheerful rhyme to reinforce color and number awareness with everyone's favorite party decoration—balloons! To prepare, cut out a felt balloon shape in each of the following colors: red, yellow, blue, and green. Arrange the balloons on a flannelboard. During circle time, read aloud the following rhyme. When appropriate, invite a different child to remove each balloon. Then put the balloons back on the flannelboard and repeat as desired, encouraging little ones to chime in as they learn the rhyme. Fun!

Four birthday balloons hanging from a tree.
[Child's name] took the red one; that left three.

Three birthday balloons—yellow, green, and blue.
[Child's name] took the yellow one; that left two.

Two birthday balloons swinging in the sun.
[Child's name] took the blue one; that left one.

One birthday balloon, left when the party was done.
[Child's name] took the green one; that left none.

Happy Birthday Book

This charming class-made book will become a treasured keepsake for each birthday child. On a child's birthday, give each youngster a sheet of paper and have him illustrate the birthday child. Then, as he dictates, write at least one thing he likes about the birthday child. Duplicate the book cover pattern on page 117 and invite the birthday child to decorate it and write her name in the space provided. Stack all the pages behind the cover and staple it along the left side to make a booklet. Present the book to the birthday child and have her take it home to share with her family. How sweet!

She plays soccer with me.

Birthday Cake

This fingerplay will really get your little partygoers in the mood for fun! Use it whenever there is a birthday in your bunch.

Birthday cake, birthday cake—   *Make stirring motion.*
Pour it in a pan.   *Make pouring motion.*
Let's bake a cake   *Pretend to put cake in oven.*
As fast as we can.   *Tap imaginary watch.*

Spread it with frosting;   *Pretend to spread frosting on cake.*
Stick the candles in.   *Pretend to put candles on cake.*
Today is [child's name]'s birthday.   *Point to birthday child.*
Now the party can begin!   *Put hands into air.*

Dramatic Play

Birthday parties are fun to plan as well as attend, so invite little ones to throw a party for a classroom pet or stuffed animal! Stock your dramatic-play area with a variety of party supplies, such as hats, mylar balloons, small cake pans, paper plates, gift boxes, frosting, ice cream containers, sales flyers from local party stores, and clean, empty cake mix boxes. Encourage a small group of students in this center to plan a birthday party and then enjoy some pretend cake and ice cream with the guest of honor.

Birthday Hat Snacks

Birthday hats are often pointy, cone-shaped, and brightly decorated. These birthday hats are also sweet, crispy, and tasty! In advance, tint several cans of vanilla frosting each with a different shade of food coloring to make bright colors. Give each child a paper plate, a sugar cone, a craft stick, access to the colored frosting, and access to Froot Loops cereal pieces. Encourage her to frost her cone with a desired shade of frosting and then press cereal pieces into the frosting to decorate the hat. When the class is finished, admire their handsome hats; then invite youngsters to munch away!

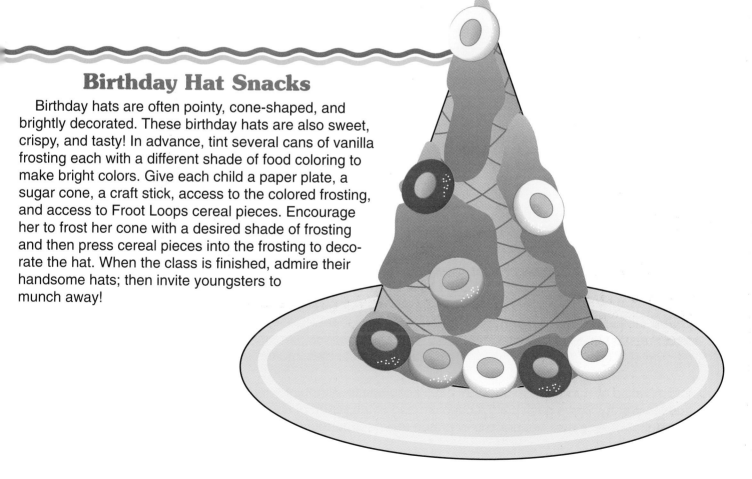

Wrapping It Up

Birthday Party

Celebrate an imaginary birthday with this festive party! You may wish to designate a classroom pet or stuffed animal as the guest of honor.

Decorations: Have students help you make and hang a colorful paper banner that says, "Happy Birthday!" If desired, use the balloons made in "Birthday Party Balloons" (page 110) and the hats made in "Party Hats" (page 110) to add pizzazz to your party.

Welcome to the Party: Get the party started by saying this rhyme aloud; then encourage your youngsters to sing the traditional birthday song afterward.

Welcome to the party.
It's about to begin.
Come and play some games.
We have prizes when you win.

Then we'll open presents
And have some little treats.
Next, we'll put on party hats
And sit down in our seats.

Out comes the birthday cake
And some ice cream too.
Now it's time for all to sing
"Happy Birthday to You."

Present Stack: Students will explore the concepts of small, medium, and large when they stack gift boxes. Encourage each child to start his stack with the largest box and then work up to the smallest box. How many boxes can he stack before they topple? If desired, give each child a small prize to reward his hard work.

Birthday Sounds: In advance, prepare a tape with familiar sounds from a birthday party. For example, record the sounds of hitting a piñata, pouring juice, a doorbell ringing, opening and closing a door, blowing out candles, and tearing wrapping paper. During the class party, play the tape and have children identify the sounds they hear.

Class Cake: Purchase a round piece of polystyrene foam to resemble a birthday cake. Also purchase birthday candles and plastic cake decorations. Let each child take a turn decorating the cake by pressing the decorations and candles into the foam.

Cake and Ice Cream: No birthday bash is complete without a serving of birthday cake and ice cream! Serve each child a cupcake and small scoop of ice cream on a birthday-patterned paper plate. A paper cup of punch makes a perfect accompaniment.

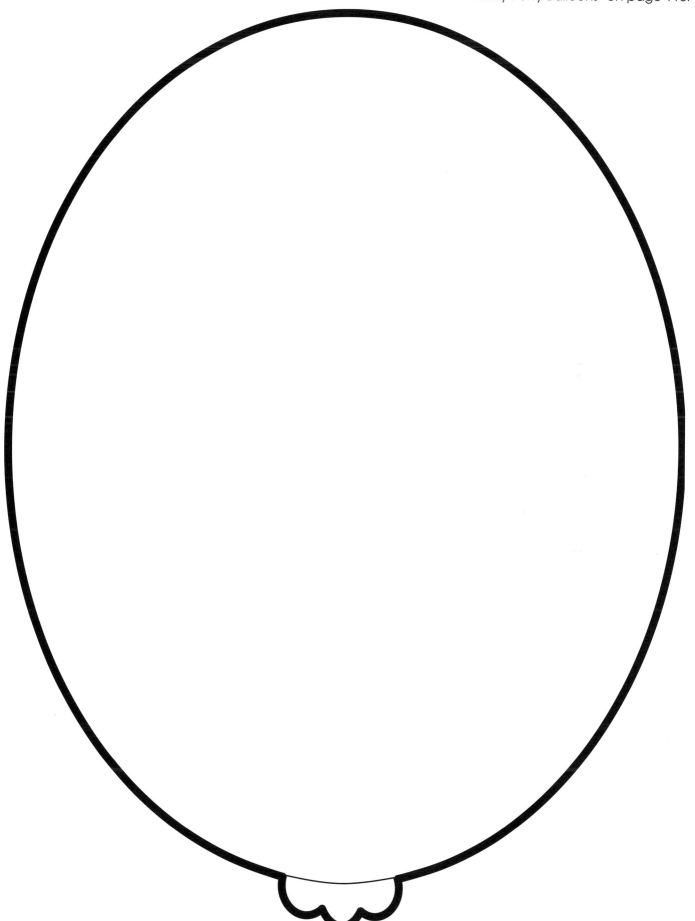

Cake and Candle Patterns
Use with "Birthday Candle Counting" on page 111.

My Favorite Things   ©The Mailbox® • *Themes on Parade* • TEC60890

Happy Birthday to

Note to the teacher: Use with "Happy Birthday Book" on page 112.

My Favorite Things 117

Teddy Bears

Tactile Teddy

Warm and fuzzy feelings are sure to arise from these tactile teddy bears. Cut out a brown construction paper copy of the bear pattern (page 123) for each child. Also gather scraps of various tactile materials such as felt, sandpaper, cellophane, satin ribbon, yarn, burlap, cotton, and fake fur. Have each child glue several different scraps onto his teddy bear. When the glue is dry, sit in a circle with youngsters and ask each child to name his bear and then describe how one of the tactile items feels.

Cinnamon Bear Puppet

Boost youngsters' awareness of the sense of smell with these "bear-y" spicy puppets! Make a white construction paper copy of page 123 for each child. Invite each child to choose a fingerpaint color and then paint her bear. Before the paint dries, have her sprinkle cinnamon on the tummy of the bear. When the paint is dry, shake off the excess cinnamon. Then cut out each bear and tape a craft stick to the back to make a puppet. If desired, invite partners to use their puppets to make up a story about the adventures of a cinnamon bear.

Color Bears

This parade of bears and balloons makes a colorful matching game. Make eight different-colored construction paper copies of the bear pattern on page 123. Program each bear with the corresponding color word and then cut the bears out. Also cut out a class supply of construction paper balloon shapes that match the bear colors. Display the bears in a row on a wall for easy access by youngsters. Gather students and help them name the color of each bear. Next, point to each bear and ask youngsters to pop up if they are wearing the clothes that match that color. Then have one child at a time choose a balloon cutout, name its color, and match it to a bear. Tape each balloon above the corresponding bear. Later, add strings to connect each set of balloons to the correct bear.

Five Little Teddy Bears

Friendly stuffed bears make counting backward "bear-y" fun! Gather students in a circle and place five stuffed teddy bears in the middle of the group. Read the rhyme shown to youngsters, inserting a child's name where indicated. With each verse, ask the named child to hop up and take one teddy bear back to her spot. Replace the bears at the end of the rhyme. Then repeat the rhyme several times until each child has had a chance to participate.

Five little teddy bears sitting in the store,
[Child's name] bought one; that left four.

Four little teddy bears as cute as they can be,
[Child's name] bought one; that left three.

Three little teddy bears with nothing to do,
[Child's name] bought one; that left two.

Two little teddy bears sitting in the sun,
[Child's name] bought one; that left one.

One little teddy bear now all alone,
It wishes that someone would take it home!

Snuggly Teddy Talk

Teddy bear hugs! Boost youngsters' confidence to speak in a group setting with help from a comforting teddy bear. Gather a variety of objects—such as toy vehicles, play food, keys, and doll clothes—and place them in a basket. Sit with youngsters in a circle and read a favorite bear story, such as *Corduroy* by Don Freeman. Next, show youngsters a snuggly teddy bear and invite them to help make up a story about the bear. Model for youngsters how to hug the bear as you draw one item from the basket. Then say a sentence out loud about the bear interacting with the item. For example, you may pull out a toy vehicle and say, "My teddy and I are driving the van to the beach." Replace the item; then have each child, in turn, repeat the activity as the bear is passed around the circle.

Teddy Bears Everywhere

Where are the teddy bears? Youngsters will practice listening skills as they search for these visiting teddy bears. While students are out of the room, place a teddy bear in each location described in the rhyme below. As you recite the rhyme, ask youngsters to point to the corresponding teddy bear.

Teddy bear on the shelf.
Teddy bear on the floor.
Teddy bear on the rug.
Teddy bear by the door.

Teddy bear in a box.
Teddy bear on a chair.
Teddy bear on the books.
Teddy bears are everywhere!

Dramatic Play

Hosting teddy's tea party is "bear-y" fun! Add several teddy bears and doll clothes to your dramatic-play center. Also stock the center with various plastic teacups, saucers, teapots, spoons, and napkins. Invite youngsters to plan a tea party for their teddy bear friends. Encourage them to dress the bears and pretend to serve tea and snacks. There's sure to be a lot of learning brewing at this party.

Teddy Bear Biscuits

These tasty teddy bears are a real treat! Give each child in a small group a refrigerated biscuit on a personalized square of oil-sprayed aluminum foil. Also allow children access to a bowl of chocolate chips and a container of cinnamon sugar. Help each child follow the directions below. Then bake the biscuits according to the package directions. If desired, serve the biscuits with honey butter or jam. Mmm!

1. Pull two small pieces of dough off the biscuit and then roll all three pieces into separate balls.
2. Flatten the largest ball to make a bear head.
3. Press the two small balls onto the head to make ears.
4. Press in chocolate chip facial features.
5. Sprinkle the face and ears with cinnamon sugar.

Dawson

Wrapping It Up

Teddy Bear Picnic

Teddy bear, teddy bear, let's have a picnic! Use the following suggestions to help plan a teddy bear picnic for youngsters and their own teddy bears. Invite each child to bring a favorite bear from home on the day of the picnic. (Have a few extras on hand for those who don't have one.)

Picnic Snack: Bring a picnic basket to school and let youngsters help pack it with snacks. Spread out blankets and invite each child and her teddy bear to gather around. Have several children unpack the picnic basket and pass out the snacks.

Picnic Song: Sing the song below as youngsters enjoy their picnic.

(sung to the tune of "Up on the Housetop")

The teddy bears went to the park to play.
They are having a picnic today.
They played ball and ran races.
They ate honey and licked their faces!
Yum, yum, yum—honey in my tum.
Yum, yum, yum—I'll have some!
The teddy bears went to the park to play.
They are having a picnic today.

Hide the Honey: Hide a plastic bear-shaped jar of honey in the classroom. Ask each child to have her teddy bear "sniff" around the room to find the honey. When the honey has been found, reward each child with a taste.

Teddy Bear Toss: In an open area, place one teddy bear on a picnic blanket. Have youngsters gather around the blanket, grasp the edge, and raise and lower their arms to gently toss the teddy bear. Repeat until each child has had an opportunity to have her teddy bear tossed.

Bear Relay: Set up a relay race in an open area outdoors. Divide students into two teams and have them stand in line holding their teddy bears. Then have each child quickly walk or hop to the designated spot and then return. Have her teddy bear tag the next teddy in line. Continue until each child and teddy bear has had a turn.

Teddy Bear Pattern

Use with "Tactile Teddy" and "Cinnamon Bear Puppet" on page 118 and "Color Bears" on page 119.

Transportation

Transportation Mobiles

Rev up classroom decor with these "wheel-y" great mobiles! For each child, cut the center from a paper plate and make a white construction paper copy of the vehicle patterns on page 129. Have each child color the vehicles and then help him cut them out. Next, punch four evenly spaced holes in the paper plate ring and hole-punch the top of each vehicle pattern. Help each child tie a length of yarn onto each vehicle cutout and then tie it onto the ring to make a mobile. Attach a yarn hanger on each mobile and display them around the classroom.

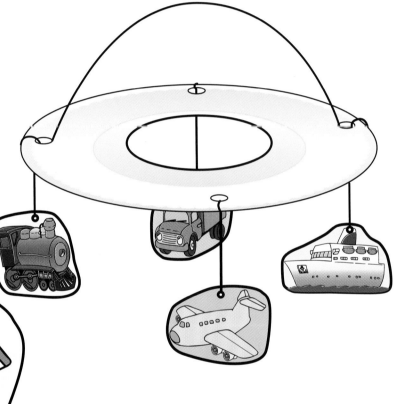

Vehicle Props

Vroom, vroom! Motoring through this vehicle parade reinforces youngsters' listening skills. Make enough white construction paper copies of page 129 for each child to have one vehicle pattern. Cut out the patterns and lay them on a table. Invite each child to choose one cutout and then color it. Help each child tape a craft stick onto the back of her pattern for a handle. Then encourage youngsters to listen as you call out directions to stop and go in a vehicle parade around the classroom. If desired, guide each child to use her prop as you sing the vehicle songs on page 128.

Toy Car Measurement

Beep, beep! This activity introduces youngsters to nonstandard measurement. Gather a collection of small same-size toy vehicles. Select several vehicles such as police cars, fire trucks, or garbage trucks, and discuss with students the jobs of people who drive those types of vehicles. Next, model for students how to place the vehicles end-to-end to measure a table. Help students count the line of vehicles. Then have student pairs work together to measure other objects around the classroom with the vehicles.

By Air, Land, and Water

This activity gets youngsters on track with sorting skills. Cut out pictures of different vehicles—including trucks, airplanes, trains, and boats—from magazines and travel brochures. Glue each picture onto a construction paper square for durability. Divide a sheet of poster board into four sections. In each section, draw one of the following: a road, clouds, a train track, or waves. Point to each section and discuss with students the type of vehicle that would travel there. Then have students sort the vehicle pictures onto the corresponding section of the poster board.

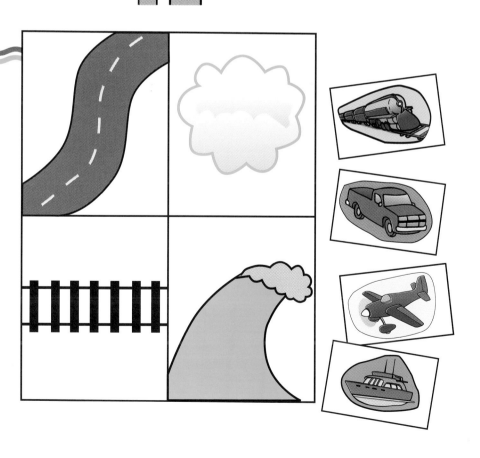

Picture Lists

Planes, trains, fire trucks, and more! Youngsters are always eager to talk about transportation vehicles. Post a sheet of chart paper labeled with a different transportation topic, such as "Trucks," "Emergency Vehicles," or "Vehicles That Fly." Ask youngsters to name different vehicles that fit into the chosen category. Record students' responses on the chart. Then invite youngsters to draw or cut out magazine pictures of corresponding vehicles and glue them onto the chart. Repeat the activity at a later time with a different transportation topic. Leave the charts displayed to refer to during your transportation study.

Trucks
pickup
dump truck
semi

Vehicles That Fly
airplane
helicopter
jet

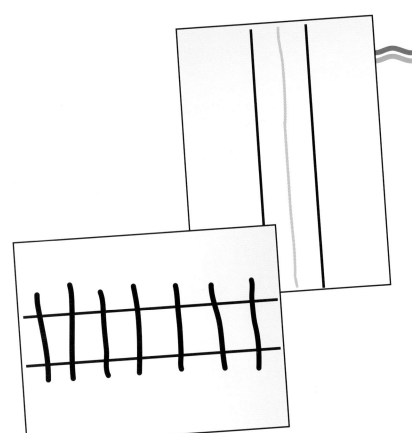

Prewriting Practice

Cruise through prewriting practice with this drawing activity. Program a sheet of paper with parallel lines. Make two copies for each child and set out yellow and black washable markers. Ask each child to draw a straight yellow line down the center of one set of vertical lines to make a street. Next, have him draw lines on the horizontal set to make a train track as shown. Then give each child vehicle stickers to add to his street and train track. Cruisin'!

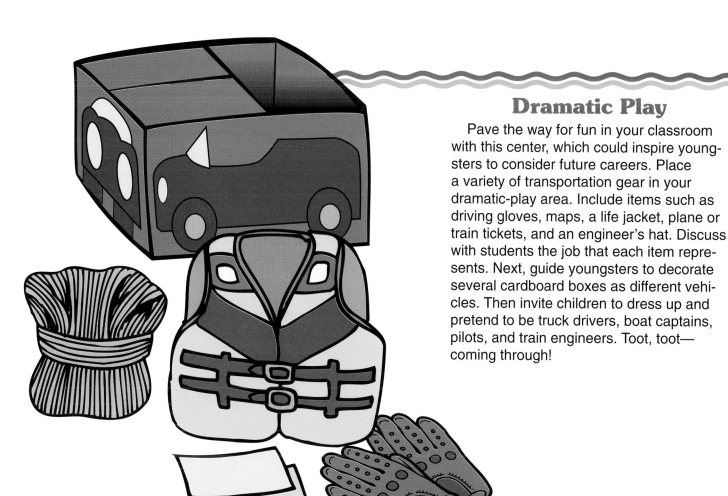

Dramatic Play

Pave the way for fun in your classroom with this center, which could inspire youngsters to consider future careers. Place a variety of transportation gear in your dramatic-play area. Include items such as driving gloves, maps, a life jacket, plane or train tickets, and an engineer's hat. Discuss with students the job that each item represents. Next, guide youngsters to decorate several cardboard boxes as different vehicles. Then invite children to dress up and pretend to be truck drivers, boat captains, pilots, and train engineers. Toot, toot—coming through!

Truck Snacks

Honk, honk! This little truck treat may be too cute to eat. Give each child a graham cracker and two small round cheese crackers on a large paper plate. Help her break her graham cracker in half and then break one square in half again. Next, help her spread frosting on the graham crackers. Have her position the crackers to make a truck shape and then add the round cracker wheels as shown. Give each child a handful of round cereal pieces to decorate her truck with. Then invite her to drive her truck around on the paper plate before enjoying her tasty treat.

Wrapping It Up

Transportation Song Posters

Surround your classroom and students with transportation songs! Display four large sheets of chart paper. Next, copy each song below on a separate chart. Then lead youngsters in singing each song to the tune of "I'm a Little Teapot." Give each child a pattern from page 129 and have him color it. Then sing the songs again and have him tape his pattern to the corresponding chart.

Songs:

I'm a Little Airplane

I'm a little airplane that flies in the sky.
I can soar way up high.
When I see another airplane, I dip to say,
"I hope you have a wonderful day."

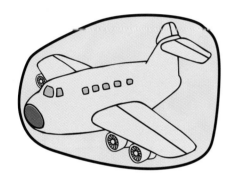

I'm a Little Truck

I'm a little truck that drives on the ground.
I haul things from town to town.
When I see another truck, I honk to say,
"I hope you have a wonderful day."

I'm a Little Boat

I'm a little boat that floats all day
In the ocean or in the bay.
When I see another boat, I toot and say,
"I hope you have a wonderful day."

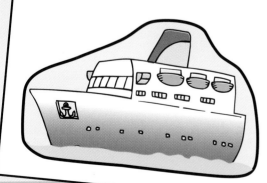

I'm a Little Train

I'm a little train that goes on a track.
First I go one way; then I come back.
When I see another train, I whistle to say,
"I hope you have a wonderful day."

Vehicle Patterns
Use with "Transportation Mobiles" and "Vehicle Puppets" on page 124 and
"Transportation Song Posters" on page 128.

Pets

Four-Legged Pets

Youngsters transform a paper cup into an adorable pet with this crafty idea! Give each youngster a nine-ounce paper cup and encourage her to paint it brown. After the paint is dry, cut out four notches in the cup, as shown, to make four legs. Give each child a small cat head cutout (see pattern shown) or dog head cutout. Encourage her to use crayons to add features. Then help her glue the head to the cup. Finally, make a hole in the bottom of the cup. Encourage each child to slide a brown pipe cleaner into the hole to resemble a tail; bend the portion of the pipe cleaner inside the cup so it stays in place. Too cute!

©The Mailbox®

Fabulous Fishbowl

These artsy fishbowls make a nifty wall display! For each child, cut two fishbowl-shaped pieces from clear Con-Tact paper. Remove the backing from one piece and place it sticky side up in front of the child. Encourage her to make colorful fish cutouts and stick them to the Con-Tact paper. Invite her to embellish the scene with other cutouts, such as seaweed, snails, and rocks. Remove the backing from the second piece of Con-Tact paper and press it over the picture, smoothing to remove the air bubbles. Display these lovely fishbowls on a wall or bulletin board.

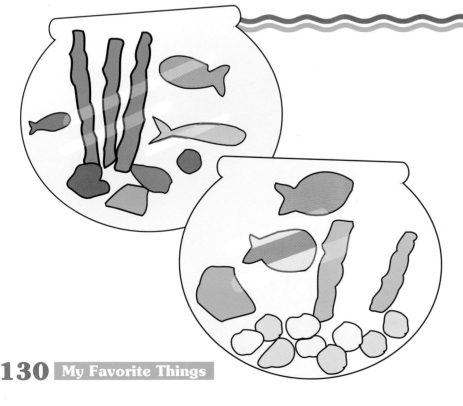

Pet Homes

Some little critters might not be happy living in a bowl of water, but a pet fish might think it's the perfect home! Youngsters match pets to their ideal homes with this center activity. Make a set of cards with a simple picture of a different pet on each one. Also make a second set of cards with a picture of each animal's home. Place both sets at a center. A child makes pairs of cards by matching each animal to its home. A hutch is the perfect home for that pet rabbit!

Fish Dominoes

Students match goldfish when they play this fun twist on the game of dominoes! Make a set of large dominoes by dividing several small index cards in half. Draw simple fish (or use a fish rubber stamp and an ink pad to make prints) on the cards in every possible number combination. Laminate the cards for durability. Then invite three youngsters to join you at a table. Place a domino faceup on the table. Divide the remaining dominoes between the youngsters. Encourage students to take turns placing dominoes with matching numbers of fish beside either end of the domino train. If a child can't make a match, she allows her teammates to play and then tries again during her next turn.

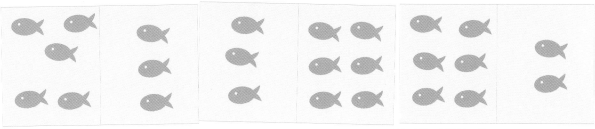

Who Am I?

These riddles are the cat's meow! When youngsters correctly identify the answer to each riddle, invite them to imitate the pet as they move about the classroom.

I like to play ball in the park.
All day long I run and bark. *(Dog)*

I'm soft and cuddly and hunt for mice.
Don't you think that mice are nice? *(Cat)*

I am yellow and love to sing.
All day long I sit in my swing. *(Bird)*

I blow bubbles and flap my fins
As round and round my bowl I swim. *(Fish)*

Little Puppy

Little ones are sure to enjoy this adaptation of a traditional rhyme.

I found a little puppy, so I took him home.
I gave him a bath and I gave him a bone.
I gave him some food and some water too.
He licked my face to say thank you.

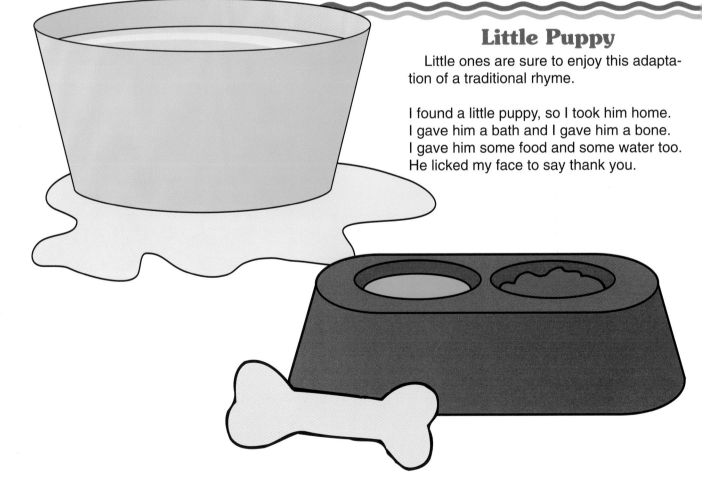

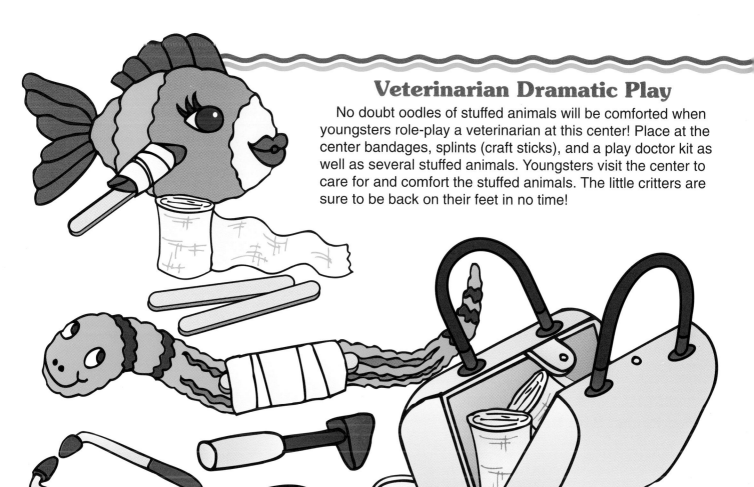

Veterinarian Dramatic Play

No doubt oodles of stuffed animals will be comforted when youngsters role-play a veterinarian at this center! Place at the center bandages, splints (craft sticks), and a play doctor kit as well as several stuffed animals. Youngsters visit the center to care for and comfort the stuffed animals. The little critters are sure to be back on their feet in no time!

Fishbowl Snack

Your little ones will be bowled over by these nifty snacks! Give each youngster a paper plate that has been cut to resemble a fishbowl as shown. Encourage a child to spread cream cheese or another tasty spread on an oval cracker and a triangular cracker and place them, as shown, to resemble a fish. If desired, invite her to place a black olive slice (eye) on the fish. Have her place a spoonful of mini M&M's (gravel) at the bottom of the bowl. Then encourage her to add two small celery sticks (seaweed). Have each student admire her handiwork before nibbling on her snack!

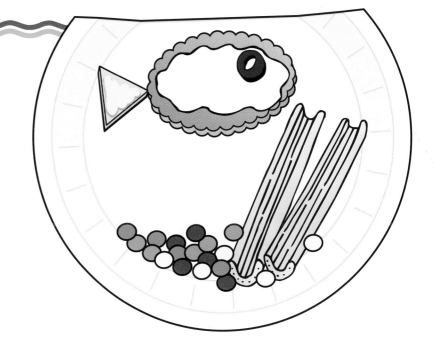

Wrapping It Up

Pet Puppets

Dogs, cats, hamsters, and fish! Using the patterns on page 135, help students make one of the pet puppets described below. Then use the puppets in centers, for sorting activities, or as props for various pet-themed songs and rhymes!

Fish Puppet With Bowl: Have the student color a copy of the fish pattern. Help her tape a craft stick to the back to make a puppet. To make a bowl for the fish, trim a large paper plate, as shown, and cut a slit in the center. Have the student color the bowl blue and add any desired embellishments. Help the child slide the puppet into the slit.

Dog Puppet With House: Have the student color a copy of the dog pattern. Help her tape a craft stick to the back to make a puppet. To make a house for the dog, trim a large paper plate, as shown, and cut a slit in the center. Encourage the student to embellish the house as desired. Help the student slide the puppet into the slit.

Cat Puppet With Pillow: Have the student color a copy of the cat pattern. Help her tape a craft stick to the back to make a puppet. To make a pillow for the cat, cut a slit in the center of a large paper plate. Encourage the student to draw cat toys on the pillow. Help the child slide the puppet into the slit.

Hamster Puppet With Cage: Have the student color a copy of the hamster pattern. Help her tape a craft stick to the back to make a puppet. To make a cage for the hamster, trim a large paper plate, as shown, and cut a slit in the center. Encourage the student to draw a water and food bowl in the cage as well as any hamster toys if desired. Help the child slide the puppet into the slit.

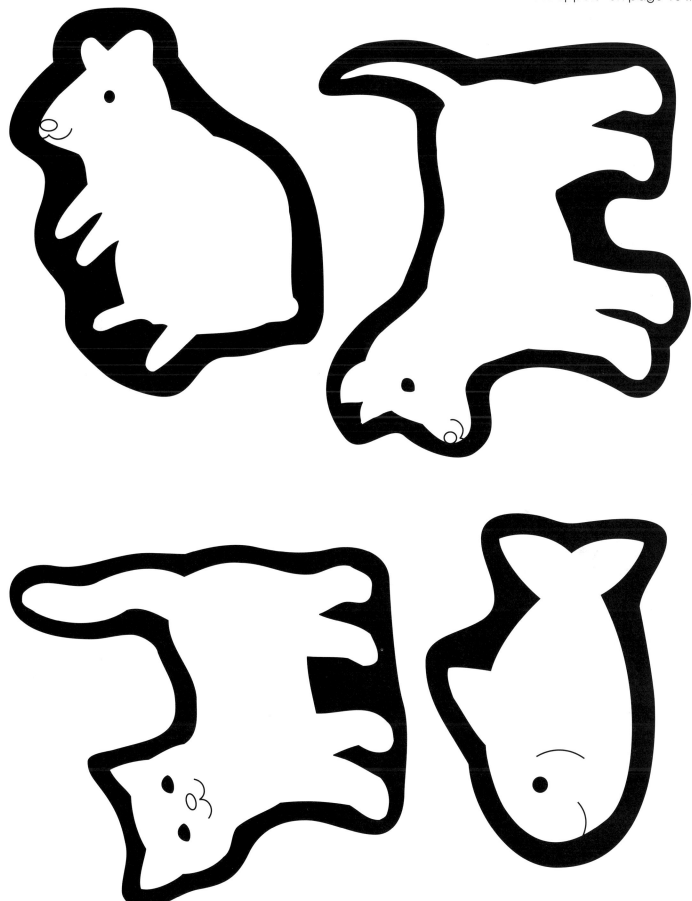

Ice Cream

Triple-Decker Cones

Set up a scoop shop in your art center! Copy the cone pattern on page 141 onto tan construction paper to make a class supply. Also copy the scoop patterns onto various shades of construction paper so that each child has three. Cut out all the patterns and store them in your art center with sheets of construction paper and glue. Working with one small group at a time, have each child, in turn, select a cone and three scoops and then glue them to a sheet of paper. If desired, have each child glue real ice-cream sprinkles to her finished cone for an eye-catching treat!

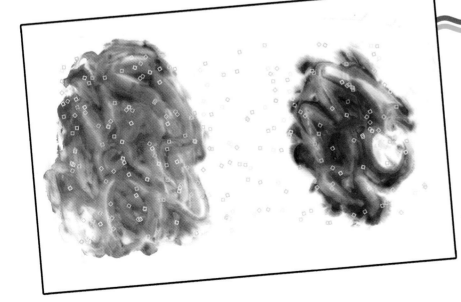

Ice-Cream Factory

Youngsters mix up an artistic batch of ice cream with this cool project. Give each child in a small group a large sheet of white paper. Invite him to paint his entire paper with white fingerpaint. Then give him a craft stick and access to bowls of red and brown fingerpaint. Invite him to use his stick to mix some red or brown paint into the white paint to resemble strawberry or chocolate ice cream. When he is satisfied with the results, encourage him to sprinkle clear glitter over his artwork. When the paint dries, it will have a frosty appearance. If desired, invite students to cut from their papers shapes that resemble scoops of ice cream, and use them in a class display.

Ice-Cream Matchup

Here's a mouthwatering matching game that's guaranteed to get youngsters interested in ice-cream treats! In advance, copy the ice-cream treat cards on pages 142–143 onto white construction paper. Cut apart and color the cards; then laminate them if desired. A pair of children mixes up the cards; then the twosome takes turns making ice-cream matches. Everyone will want a second helping!

Ice-Cream Relay

Ready, set, scoop! Have students form two lines. Give the first child in each line an ice-cream cone and a tennis ball (scoop of ice cream). Have him place the scoop atop his cone. At your signal, the child walks to a designated spot, turns around, and returns to his line. He passes the cone to the next child in line. If at any time the scoop falls off the cone, the child must stop and put it back on top. Play continues in this manner, with each child taking a turn. At the end of the relay, congratulate your super scoopers on a job well done!

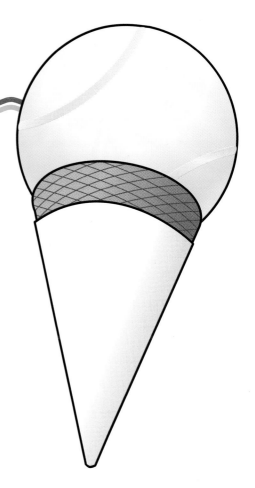

Describing Ice-Cream

Stack these descriptive scoops for a sweet introduction to describing words! Copy the scoop patterns on page 141 onto construction paper to make a supply. Cut out the scoops and store them in your circle-time area. Also copy the cone pattern on page 141 onto tan paper; then cut it out and post it on the back of your classroom door. Gather youngsters and ask them to think of words to tell about ice cream. As volunteers give suggestions, write each word on a different scoop. Tape each word above the cone to form a tall ice-cream cone. Read the words aloud and review them each time students line up at the door.

frozen
good
icy
wet
sticky
cold
sweet

Alyson likes strawberry ice cream.

We Like Ice Cream!

Ice-Cream Stories

This shaped booklet is just right for an ice-cream story! Program a class supply of paper plates with "_____ likes _____ ice cream." Help each child write her name in the first blank and her favorite ice-cream flavor in the second blank. Then encourage her to illustrate on her plate a picture of herself eating ice cream. Bind the finished pages and attach the last plate to a tagboard ice-cream dish as shown. Write a title on the dish and read the completed booklet with your students. We all scream for ice cream!

I mad grp chp.

Ice-Cream Lab

Invite your little ice-cream creators to make up new flavors in this tasty dramatic-play center! Stock a center with paper bowls, plastic spoons, ice-cream scoops, aprons, and clean, empty ice-cream and topping containers. Invite a small group of students to this center to pretend to work at an ice-cream company creating new flavors of ice cream. Encourage students to use the props as they imagine new ice-cream flavors. Provide paper and crayons for youngsters to use to draw and write about their creations. How many different flavors will they create today?

Kick-the-Can Ice Cream

It's time to make a batch of fresh, delicious ice cream! This outdoor method requires students to use their hands—and feet! In advance, follow the recipe below to prepare ice-cream mix for each group of four students. Place each bag of mix inside a large metal coffee can. Fill the can with layers of ice and rock salt. Put the lid on the can and tape the edges for added security. Take students outside to a flat area of the playground. Provide each group with a prepared can and have them gently roll and kick the can to each other for approximately 15 minutes. At five-minute intervals, check each can and add ice and salt as needed. When the ice cream is frozen, remove the bag from the can; rinse the outside of the bag with cold water and let each group feel it. Cut off one corner of the bag and squeeze the treat into paper cups. Now that's some frosty fun!

Ice-Cream Mix
(serves four)
1 c. whole milk
1 c. half-and-half
½ tsp. vanilla extract
½ c. sugar
Pour the ingredients into a quart-size freezer bag. Force out all the air, seal the bag, and reinforce the seal with duct tape. Freeze as directed above.

Ice-Cream Parlor

Set up a classroom ice-cream parlor. Cover small tables with red-and-white checkered tablecloths. Then supply paper bowls, plastic spoons, napkins, ice-cream scoops, and clean, empty ice-cream and topping containers. If desired, provide paper cones and large pom-poms in a variety of colors to resemble scoops of ice cream.

Sign Making: Every ice-cream parlor needs a sign! Put your little ones to work thinking of a name for the ice-cream parlor. Then help them make a large sign on poster board or a length of bulletin board paper. Hang the completed sign over your ice-cream parlor.

Super-Scooper Hats: Outfit each little scooper with one of these adorable hats! Cut out a construction paper headband for each child. Also cut out a class supply of tan construction paper triangles (cones) and pastel construction paper circles (scoops). Have each child glue a scoop atop a cone and then glue the ice-cream cone to the center of his headband. If desired, help him write his name on the side. Then, when the glue is dry, tape the ends to finish the headband.

Tasty Treats: Invite each little scooper to take a turn serving ice cream to classmates. Have him use an ice-cream scoop to put pom-poms into a bowl. Then he squirts on some pretend toppings and serves it with a smile.

I Love Ice Cream: While youngsters enjoy their ice-cream parlor, encourage them to sing this song.

(sung to the tune of "Three Blind Mice")

I love ice cream.
I love ice cream.
Yes, I do.
Yes, I do.
I love ice-cream bars; don't you?
I love ice-cream sundaes too.
I love ice-cream cones; yes, I do.
I love ice cream.

Little Ones' Ice-Cream Parlor

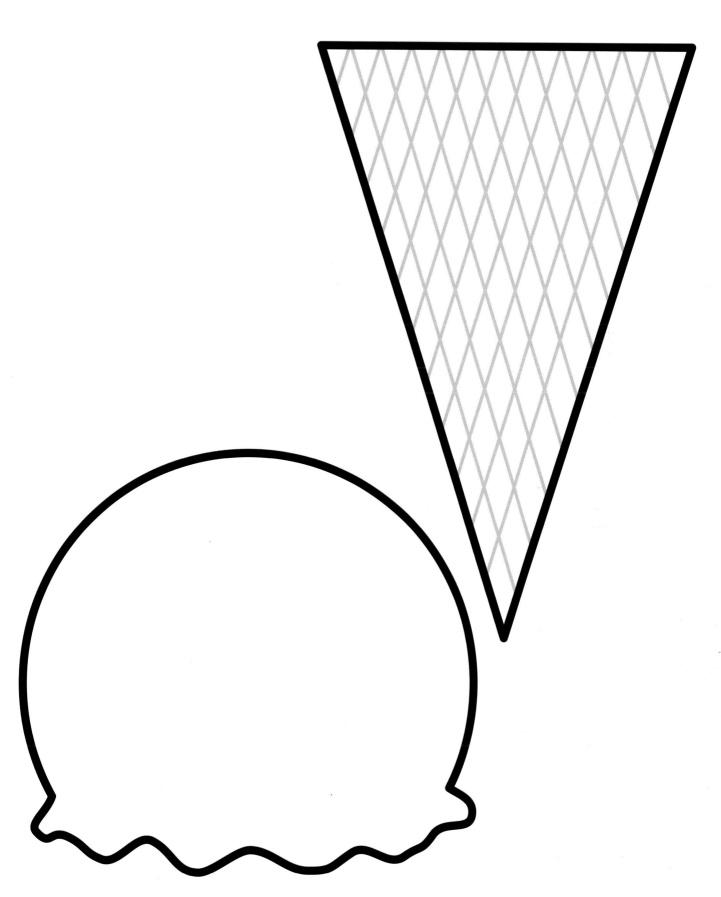

Ice-Cream Treat Cards

Use with "Ice-Cream Matchup" on page 137.

My Favorite Things Parade

Plan a Favorite Things Parade with youngsters. Invite them to carry favorite toys or play foods to represent their favorite foods. Have students wear their bracelets from "Friendship Bracelets" on page 104, carry their balloon projects from "Birthday Party Balloon" on page 110, or hold their ice-cream cone projects from "Triple-Decker Cones" on page 136. Then teach youngsters the song below and let the parade begin!

My Favorite Things Parade Song

(sung to the tune of "When Johnny Comes Marching Home")

The children are marching into town. Hooray! Hooray!
The children are marching in a Favorite Things parade.
Some have pets, and some have toys.
All have friends, both girls and boys.
Oh, we're so glad the children could come today.

The children are marching into town. Hooray! Hooray!
The children are marching in a Favorite Things parade.
They love ice cream and birthdays too.
Some snuggle a bear; it is true.
Oh, we're so glad the children could come today.